The Fantasticks
Celebration

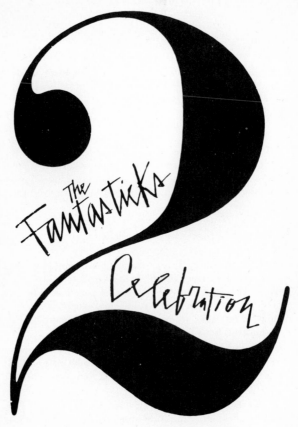

Musicals by Tom Jones and Harvey Schmidt

DRAMA BOOK SPECIALISTS/PUBLISHERS

New York

Library of Congress Cataloging in Publication Data
Schmidt, Harvey.
    The Fantasticks. Celebration.
    Librettos; music by Schmidt.
    1. Musical revues, comedies, etc.—Librettos. I. Schmidt, Harvey.
Celebration. Libretto. English. 1973. II. Jones, Tom, librettist. The Fantasticks.
III. Jones, Tom, librettist. Celebration. IV. Title. V. Title: Celebration.
ML49.S33F3   782.8'1'2   73-5972   ISBN 0-910482-44-6

Printed in U.S.A. by
NOBLE OFFSET PRINTERS, INC.
New York, N.Y. 10003

The Fantasticks

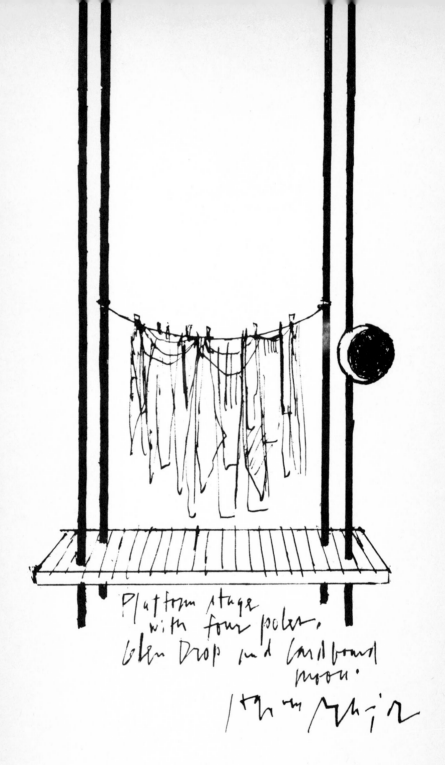

Platform stage with four poles, leaf drop and cardboard moon.

Drawing by HARVEY SCHMIDT of the Sullivan Street stage.

The Fantasticks

Words by
Tom Jones

Music by
Harvey Schmidt

Suggested by a play
LES ROMANESQUES
by Edmund Rostand

For B. Iden Payne

Top: JERRY ORBACH. Middle, left to right: HUGH THOMAS, RITA GARDNER, WILLIAM LARSEN. Bottom, left to right: RICHARD STAUFFER, KENNETH NELSON, GEORGE CURLEY.

Original Cast

THE FANTASTICKS was first presented by Lore Noto at the Sullivan Street Playhouse, New York City, on May 3rd, 1960, with the following cast:

THE MUTE . . . . Richard Stauffer

EL GALLO . . . . Jerry Orbach

LUISA . . . . Rita Gardner

MATT . . . . Kenneth Nelson

HUCKLEBEE . . . . William Larsen

BELLOMY . . . . Hugh Thomas

HENRY . . . . Thomas Bruce

MORTIMER . . . . George Curley

THE HANDYMAN . . . . Jay Hampton

* * *

THE PIANIST . . . . Julian Stein
THE HARPIST . . . . Beverly Mann

Directed by WORD BAKER
Musical Director and Arrangements by
JULIAN STEIN
Production designed by ED WITTSTEIN

Associate Producers
SHELLY BARON, DOROTHY OLIM,
ROBERT ALAN GOLD

Cast of the very first one-act version of THE FANTASTICKS presented at Mildred Dunnock's
BARNARD SUMMER THEATRE, August 1959. Left to right: GEORGE MORGAN, DICK BURNHAM,
LEE CROGHAN, SUSAN WATSON, JONATHAN FARWELL, CRAYTON ROWE,
RON LEIBMAN, BILL TOST.

Musical Numbers

ACT ONE

OVERTURE	The Company
TRY TO REMEMBER	El Gallo
MUCH MORE	Luisa
METAPHOR	Matt and Luisa
NEVER SAY "NO"	Hucklebee and Bellomy
IT DEPENDS ON WHAT YOU PAY	El Gallo, Bellomy, and Hucklebee
SOON IT'S GONNA RAIN	Matt and Luisa
THE RAPE BALLET	The Company
HAPPY ENDING	Matt, Luisa, Hucklebee and Bellomy

ACT TWO

THIS PLUM IS TOO RIPE	Matt, Luisa, Hucklebee and Bellomy
I CAN SEE IT	El Gallo and Matt
PLANT A RADISH	Hucklebee and Bellomy
ROUND & ROUND	El Gallo, Luisa and Company
THEY WERE YOU	Matt and Luisa
TRY TO REMEMBER (REPRISE)	El Gallo

COLIN RUSSELL as the Mute
in the Dublin, Ireland production.

Act I

*T*his play should be played on a platform. There is no scenery, but occasionally a stick may be held up to represent a wall. Or a cardboard moon may be hung upon a pole to indicate that it's night. When the audience enters the auditorium, the platform is clearly in sight, and there is a tattered drape across the front of it upon which is lettered "The Fantasticks."

During the Overture, the members of the Company arrive and prepare to do the play. They take down the lettered drape, set out the Prop Box, and put the finishing touches on their costumes. When the music is over, they take their places and wait while the Narrator (El Gallo) sings to the audience.

EL G: *Sings.*

Try to remember the kind of September
When life was slow and oh, so mellow.
Try to remember the kind of September
When grass was green and grain was yellow.
Try to remember the kind of September
When you were a tender and callow fellow.
Try to remember, and if you remember,
Then follow.

LUISA: Follow, follow, follow, follow.

EL G: Try to remember when life was so **tender**
That no one wept except the willow.
Try to remember when life was so tender
That dreams were kept beside your pillow.
Try to remember when life was so tender
That love was an ember about to billow.

11

Try to remember, and if you remember,
Then follow.

LUISA: Follow, follow, follow, follow.
MATT: Follow, follow, follow, follow.
FATHERS: Follow, follow, follow, follow.

EL G: Deep in December, it's nice to remember,
Although you know the snow will follow.
Deep in December, it's nice to remember:
Without a hurt the heart is hollow.
Deep in December, it's nice to remember
The fire of September that made us mellow.
Deep in December, our hearts should remember,
And follow.

Speaks to audience.

Let me tell you a few things you may want to know
Before we begin the play.
First of all, the characters:
A boy; A girl; Two fathers;
And a wall.
Anything else that's needed
We can get from out this box.

MUTE displays Prop Box.

It's hard to know which is most important,
Or how it all began.
The Boy was born.
The Girl was born.
They grew up, quickly.
Went to school,
Became shy,
(In their own ways and for different reasons),

12

Read Romances,
Studied cloud formations in the lazy afternoon,
And instead of reading textbooks,
Tried to memorize the moon.
And when the girl was fifteen
(She was younger than the boy),
She began to notice something strange.
Her ugly duckling features
Had undergone a change.
In short, she was growing pretty;
For the first time in her whole life—pretty.
And the shock so stunned and thrilled her
That she became
Almost immediately
Incurably insane.
Observe:

LUISA: The moon turns red on my birthday every year and
it always will until somebody saves me and takes me
back to my palace.

EL G: That is a typical remark.
The other symptoms vary.
She thinks that she's a princess;
That her name must be in French,
Or sometimes Eurasian,
Although she isn't sure what that is.

LUISA: You see, no one can feel the way I feel
And have a father named Amos Babcock Bellomy.

EL G: She has a glue-paste necklace
Which she thinks is really real.

LUISA: I found it in the attic
With my Mother's name inside;
It is my favourite possession.

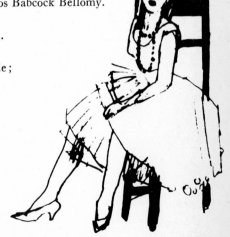

13

CARLA HUSTON as Luisa, drawing by HARVEY SCHMIDT.

EL G: It's her fancy.
LUISA: It's my pride.

This morning a bird woke me up.
It was a lark or a peacock,
Or something like that.
Some strange sort of bird that I'd never heard.
And I said "hello."
And it vanished: flew away.
The very minute that I said "hello."
It was mysterious
So do you know what I did?
I went over to my mirror
And brushed my hair two hundred times
Without stopping.
And as I was brushing it,
My hair turned gold!
No, honestly! Gold!
And then red.
And then sort of a deep blue when the sun hit it.
I'm sixteen years old,
And every day something happens to me.
I don't know what to make of it.
When I get up in the morning to get dressed,
I can tell:
Something's different.
I like to touch my eyelids
Because they're never quite the same.

Oh! Oh! Oh!
I hug myself till my arms turn blue,
Then I close my eyes and I cry and cry
Till the tears come down
And I taste them. Ah!

I love to taste my tears!
I am special.
I am special.
Please, God, please—
Don't let me be normal!

And, rapturously, SHE sings.

I'd like to swim in a clear blue stream
Where the water is icy cold;
Then go to town in a golden gown,
And have my fortune told.
Just once.
Just once.
Just once before I'm old.

ALICE CANNON as Luisa
and DAVID CRYER as
El Gallo, Sullivan Street
production, drawing by
WILLIAM AUERBACH-
LEVY.

RITA GARDNER as Luisa
in the original Sullivan
Street production

I'd like to be—not evil,
But a little worldly wise.
To be the kind of girl designed
To be kissed upon the eyes.
I'd like to dance till two o'clock,
Or sometimes dance till dawn,
Or if the band could stand it,
Just go on and on and on!
Just once.
Just once.
Before the chance is gone!

I'd like to waste a week or two,
And never do a chore.
To wear my hair unfastened
So it billows to the floor.
To do the things I've dreamed about
But never done before!
Perhaps I'm bad, or wild, or mad,
With lots of grief in store,
But I want much more than keeping house!
Much more!
Much more!
Much more!

EL G: Good.
       And now the boy.
       His story may be a wee bit briefer,
       Because it's pretty much the same.
MATT: There is this girl.
EL G: That is the essence.
MATT: There is this girl.
EL G: I warn you: it may be monotonous.

16

Original costume design for
Luisa by ED WITTSTEIN

MATT: There is this girl.
I'm nearly twenty years old.
I've studied Biology.
I've had an education.
I've been inside a lab:
Dissected violets.
I know the way things are.
I'm grown-up; stable;
Willing to conform.
I'm beyond such foolish notions,
And yet—in spite of my knowledge—
There is this girl.
She makes me young again, and foolish,
And with her I perform the impossible:
I defy Biology!
And achieve ignorance!
There are no other ears but hers to hear
the explosion of my soul! There are no other eyes

17

but hers to make me wise, and despite what they say of species, there is not one plant or animal or any growing thing that is made quite the same as she is. It's stupid, of course, I know it. And immensely undignified, but I do love her!

EL G: Look! There is the wall their fathers built between their houses.

MUTE holds up stick.

MATT: They built it ages ago last month when I came home from school. Poor fools, they built it to keep us apart. Maybe she's there now. I hope so—I'll see. . . . I don't know what to call her. She's too vibrant for a name. What shall I call her? Juliet?

LUISA: Yes, dear!

MATT: Helena?

LUISA: Yes, dear!

MATT: And Cassandra. And Cleopatra. And Beatrice. And also Guinevere?

LUISA: What, dear?

MATT: I think she's there.
Can you hear me?

LUISA: Barely.

MATT: I've been speaking of you.

LUISA: To whom?

MATT: To them—I told them that if someone were to ask me to describe you I would be utterly and totally speechless, except to say perhaps that you are Polaris or the inside of a leaf.

LUISA: Speak a little louder.

MATT: *Sings.*

I love you!

SHE swoons.

MATT: *Singing vigorously.*

If I were in the desert deep in sand, and
The sun was burning like a hot pomegranate:
Walking through a nightmare in the heart of
A summer day, until my mind was parch-ed!
Then you are water!
Cool clear water!
A refreshing glass of water!

LUISA: What, dear?

MATT: *Water!*

SHE swoons.

MATT: *Sings.*

Love! You are love!
Better far than a metaphor
Can ever ever be.
Love! You are love!
My mystery—of love!

If the world was like an iceberg,
And everything was frozen,
And tears turned into icicles in the eye!
And snow came pouring—sleet and ice—
Came stabbing like a knife!
Then you are heat!
A fire alive with heat!
A flame that thaws the iceberg with its heat!

LUISA: Repeat.

MATT: *You are heat!*

CAROLE DEMAS as Luisa,
FRANK GERACI as the Mute,
and ERIC HOWELL as Matt,
Sullivan Street production.

SHE swoons; then revives immediately to join him in song.

Love! You are love! (I am love!)
Better far than a metaphor
Can ever ever be.
Love! You are love! (I am love!)
My mystery—(his mystery) of love!

You are Polaris, the one trustworthy star!
You are! (I am!) You are! (I am!)
You are September, a special mystery
To me! (To he!) To me! (To he!)
You are Sunlight! Moonlight!
Mountains! Valleys!
The microscopic inside of a leaf!
My joy! My grief!
My star! My leaf!
Oh—

BOTH: Love! You are love! (I am love!)
Better far than a metaphor
Can ever ever be!
Love! You are love! (I am love!)
My mystery—(his mystery)
Of love!

And THEY reach over the top of the stick, and embrace.

London production, left to right: STEPHANIE VOSS as Luisa, Director WORD BAKER, MELVIN HAYES as the Mute, PETER GILMORE as Matt.

LUISA: Matt!
MATT: Luisa!
LUISA: Shh. Be careful.
        I thought I heard a sound.
MATT: But you're trembling!
LUISA: My father loves to spy.
MATT: I know; I know.
        I had to climb out through a window.
        My father locked my room.
LUISA: Oh God, be careful!
        Suppose you were to fall!
MATT: It's on the ground floor.
LUISA: Oh.
MATT: Still, the window's very small.
        I could get stuck.

LUISA: This is madness, isn't it?
MATT: Yes, it's absolutely mad!
LUISA: And also very wicked?
MATT: Yes.
LUISA: I'm glad.
MATT: My father would be furious if he knew.
LUISA: Listen, I have had a vision.
MATT: Of disaster?
LUISA: No. Of azaleas.
        I dreamed I was picking azaleas.
        When all at once, this Duke—
        Oh, he was very old,
        I'd say he was nearly forty.
        But attractive.
        And very evil.
MATT: I hate him!
LUISA: And he had a retinue of scoundrels,

21

	And they were hiding behind the rhododendrons,
	And then, all at once,
	As I picked an azalea—
	He lept out!
MATT:	God, I hate him!
LUISA:	In my vision, how I struggled.
	Like the Rape of the Sabine Women!
	I cried "help."
MATT:	And I was nearby!
LUISA:	Yes. You come rushing to the rescue.
	And, single-handed, you fight all his men,
	And win—
MATT:	And then—
LUISA:	Celebration!
MATT:	Fireworks!
LUISA:	Fiesta!
MATT:	Laughter!
LUISA:	Our fathers give in!
MATT:	We live happily ever after!
LUISA:	There's no reason in the world why it can't happen exactly like that.

Suddenly SHE stiffens.

	Someone's coming!
MATT:	It's my father.
LUISA:	Kiss me!

THEY kiss as MUSIC begins and HUCKLEBEE comes in with pruning shears and prunes away at a massive imaginary plant.

| HUCK: | Too much moisture! |

To audience.

There are a great many things I could tell you about myself. I was once in the Navy; that's where I learned Horticulture. Yes, I have been the world over. I've seen it all: mountain cactus, the century plant, Japanese Ivy. And exotic ports where bogwort was sold in the open market! I'm a man of experience and there is one thing that I've learned: Too much moisture is worse than none at all. Prune a plant. Avoid water. And go easy on manure. Moderation. That's the moral. Hmm. That's my son's foot.

MATT: Hello, Father.
HUCK: What are you doing up in that tree?
MATT: Reading verses.
HUCK: Curses.
MATT: How's that?
HUCK: I offer a father's curses
To the kind of education
That makes our children fools.
I sent this boy to school—to college;
And I hope you know what that costs.
Did he learn to dig a cesspool, no.
He's up there reading verse.
Why do I always find you
Standing beside that wall?

23

MATT: I'm waiting for it to fall.
Besides, I like it.
I like its lovely texture,
And its pretty little eyes.

HUCK: Walls don't have eyes!

MATT: Then what do you call this flower?

LUISA: Sweet God, he's clever!

HUCK: Son, you are an ass. There you sit every day, reading verses, while who knows what our neighbor is up to on the other side of that wall. He's a villain. I'll not have it! I'll strip down those branches where an enemy could climb! I'll lime that wall with bottles! I'll jag it up with glass!

LUISA: Ahh!

HUCK: What was that?

MATT: Some broken willow—some little wounded bird.

HUCK: Maybe. But walls have ears even though they don't have eyes. I'll just take a look.

Starts to climb and then stops.

Ahh! There's that stiffness. The result of my Navy career. Here, son, you climb. You can see for me.

MATT: All right, Father.

HUCK: What do you see?

MATT: I love you.

LUISA: I love you, too.

HUCK: What are you mumbling about? Get down from there if there's nothing to be seen! Down I say.

MATT: I obey.

HUCK: You're an idiot. I've decided you need to be married. So I went shopping this morning and picked you out a wife.

LUISA:	Ahh!
HUCK:	There's that sound again.
MATT:	Anguished bird.
HUCK:	Weeping willow?
	It may be.
	But let's get back to business:
	Son, I've picked you out a pearl.
MATT:	And if I prefer a diamond?
HUCK:	How dare you prefer a diamond
	When I've just offered you a pearl!
MATT:	Listen carefully to what I have to say.
	Listen, Wall. And flowers. And willow, too.
	And wounded bird. And Father, you
	May as well listen too.
	I will not wed by your wisdom.
	I will not walk neatly into a church
	And contract out to prolongate my race.
	I will not go wedding in a too-tight suit
	Nor be witnessed when I take my bride.
	No!

Music as HE speaks.

I'll marry, when I marry,
In my own particular way;
And my bride shall dress in sunlight,
With rain for her wedding veil.
Out in the open,
With no one standing by.
No song except September
Being sung in the busy grass!
No sound except our heartbeats, roaring!
Like a flower alive with bees!

25

Mexico City: ANTONIO GAMA as Matt,
ORTIZ DE PINEDO as Hucklebee.

Without benefit of neighbor!
Without benefit of book!
Except perhaps her handprint
As she presses her hand in mine;
Except perhaps her imprint
As she gives me her golden hair;
In a field, while kneeling,
Being joined by the joy of life!
There!
In the air!
In the open!
That's how I plan to wive!

HUCK: Son, you need pruning. Come inside and write SIMPLICITY two hundred times without stopping. Perhaps that will improve your style.

MATT and HUCKLEBEE exit. MUSIC as BELLOMY enters on his side, carrying an enormous watering pail with a long spout.

Original costume design for Bellomy by
ED WITTSTEIN

BELL: That's right, drink away. Open up your thirsty little mouths.

To audience.

I'm her father. And believe me, it isn't easy. Perhaps that's why I love vegetables. So dependable. You plant a radish, and you know what you're about. You don't get a turnip or a cabbage, no. Plant a turnip, get a turnip; plant a cabbage, get a cabbage. While with children—I thought I had planted a turnip or at worst perhaps an avocado: something remotely useful. I'm a merchant—I sell buttons. What need do I have for a rose?—There she is. Missy, you must go inside.

LUISA: I've told you; I'm a princess.

BELL: You're a button-maker's daughter. Now, go inside as you're told. Our enemy is beyond that wall. Up to something: I can feel it! Him and his no-good son. Look out, you've stepped in my peppers. That settles it. I'll put a fence here by this wall. A high fence, with barbed stickers! An arsenal of wire!

LUISA: A fence is expensive, Papa.

BELL: Expensive? Well, I'll build it'myself. Go inside; do as I tell you!
Is she gone?—Ha, yes—she's gone.

Yodels.

Oh lady le di le da loo!

HE puts his hand to his ear and we hear in the distance an answering yodel. BELLOMY yips with delight and rushes over to the bench as HUCKLE-BEE does the same on his side. THEY scramble up the bench and noisily embrace over the "wall."

BELL: Hucklebee!
HUCK: Bellomy!
BELL: Neighbor!
HUCK: Friend!
BELL: How's the gout?
HUCK: I barely notice. And your asthma?
BELL: A trifle.

Coughs.

I endure it.
HUCK: Well, it's nearly settled.
BELL: What is?
HUCK: The marriage. They're nearly ready. I hid in the bushes to listen. Oh, it's something; They're out of their minds with love!
BELL: Hurray.
HUCK: My son—he is fantastic!
BELL: My daughter is fantastic, too.
They're both of them mad.
HUCK: They are geese!
BELL: It was a clever plan we had.
To build this wall.
HUCK: Yes. And to pretend to feud.
BELL: Just think if they knew
That we wanted them wed.

HUGH THOMAS as the
original Bellomy, drawing by
HARVEY SCHMIDT

HUCK: A pre-arranged marriage—
BELL: They'd rather be dead!

MUSIC.

HUCK: Children!
BELL: Lovers!
HUCK: Fantasticks!
BELL: Geese!
HUCK: How clever we are.
BELL: How crafty to know.
HUCK: To manipulate children,   *manipulate*
BELL: You merely say "no."

And THEY sing.

Ohhhhhhhh—
Dog's got to bark; a mule's got to bray.
Soldiers must fight and preachers must pray.
And children, I guess, must get their own way
The minute that you say no.

Why did the kids pour jam on the cat?   *Reverse*
Raspberry jam all over the cat?   *psychology*
Why should the kids do something like that,
When all that we said was "No"?

HUCK: My son was once afraid to swim;
The water made him wince.
Until I said he mustn't swim;
'S been swimmin' ever since!

BOTH: 'S been swimmin' ever since!

Ohhhhhhhhh—
Dog's got to bark; A mule's got to bray.
Soldiers must fight and preachers must pray.

29

And children, I guess, must get their own way
The minute that you say no.

Why did the kids put beans in their ears?
No one can hear with beans in their ears.
After a while the reason appears.
They did it 'cause we said "No."

BELL: Your daughter brings a young man in,
Says 'Do you like him, Pa?'
Just tell her he's a fool and then,
You've got a son-in-law!

BOTH: You've got a son-in-law!

Ohhhhhhhhhhhhhh—
Sure as a June comes right after May!
Sure as the night comes right after day!
You can be sure the devil's to pay,
The minute that you say no.
Make sure you never say—
No!

Tokyo, Japan. Atelier 41 production, directed by TAKAO NAKAMURA,
left to right: MASANORI TOMOTAKE as Bellomy, MICHINOSUKE
SAKAGAMI as the Mute, JUN KONDO as Hucklebee.

BELL: But there's one problem left.
HUCK: How to end the feud?
BELL: Exactly; you guessed it.
We mustn't let them know.
HUCK: Oh no, if they knew—
We're finished.
BELL: We're through.
HUCK: I think I've found the answer.
It's delicious. Very theatrical.
BELL: Tell me.
HUCK: An abduction!
BELL: Who's abducted?
HUCK: Your daughter.
BELL: Who abducts her?
HUCK: A professional abductor.
I've hired the very man!

Enter EL GALLO, with a flourish.

EL G: Gentlemen, good evening.
HUCK: What the devil?
BELL: Who are you?
EL G: I was sent for.
A maiden in distress.
HUCK: Of course, you are El Gallo.
HE pronounces it American—
Gal-oh.
EL G: *HE pronounces it Spanish—*
Gayo.
HUCK: Oh—si, si.

To BELLOMY.

See, this is what I was about to tell you. We hire
this man to assist us. He starts to kidnap your daughter. My son runs in to save her. Then, a battle.

EL G: I allow the boy to defeat me . . .

HUCK: My son becomes a hero . . . and the feud is over
forever.

BELL: How much for such a drama?

EL G: That, Señor, depends.

BELL: On what?

EL G: What else? The quality of the Rape.

BELL: No.

HE starts to leave, but THEY catch him.

EL G: Forgive me. The attempted Rape. I know you prefer
Abduction, but the proper word is Rape. It's short
and businesslike.

HUCK: I heard her speak of Sabine Women.

BELL: Well, it doesn't sound right to me!

EL G: It is though, I assure you.
As a matter of fact, it's standard.
The lovers meet in secret. And so forth.
A group of villains interrupt them. And so forth.
The boy fights off pirates, Indians, bandits.
The parents relent. Happy ending. And so forth.
All of it quite standard.

BELL: What about the cost?

EL G: Cost goes by type. In your case, I think I would
recommend a "First Class."

BELL: You mean we get a choice?

EL G: Yes, of course. With regular Union rates.

32

Sings.

Rape!
R-a-a-a-pe!
Raa-aa-aa-pe!
A pretty rape.
Such a pretty rape!

We've the obvious open schoolboy rape,
With little mandolins and perhaps a cape,
The rape by coach; it's little in request.
The rape by day; but the rape by night is best.

Just try to see it,
And you will soon agree, Señors,
Why invite regret,

When you can get the sort of rape
You'll never ever forget!

You can get the rape emphatic.
You can get the rape polite.
You can get the rape with Indians,
A truly charming sight.
You can get the rape on horseback,
They all say it's new and gay.
So you see the sort of rape
Depends on what you pay.
It depends on what you pay.

> HUCK: The kids will love it.
> It depends on what you—
> BELL: Pay!
> HUCK: So why be stingy,
> It depends on what you—

RICARDO MONTALBA
as El Gallo in the
Hallmark Hall of Fame
television production.

EL G: The spectacular rape,
With costumes ordered from the East.
Requires rehearsal
And takes a dozen men at least.
A couple of singers
And a string quartet.
A major production—requires a set.

Just try to see it,
And you will soon sí, sí, Señor,
Why invite regret,
When you can get the sort of rape
You'll never ever forget!

You can get the rape emphatic.
You can get the rape polite.

You can get the rape with Indians:
A truly charming sight!
You can get the rape on horseback,
They all say it's distingué!
So you see the sort of rape
Depends on what you pay.
It depends on what you pay.

HUCK: So why be stingy.
           It depends on what you—
BELL: Pay, pay, pay!
HUCK: The kids will love it;
           It depends on what you—

EL G: The comic rape!
Perhaps it's just a trifle too unique. (Ha ha)
Romantic rape.
Done while canoeing on a moonlit creek.
The Gothic rape!
I play Valkyrie on a bass bassoon!
The drunken rape!
It's done completely in a cheap saloon.
The rape Venetian—needs a blue lagoon.
The rape with moonlight—or without a moon.
Moonlight is expensive but it's in demand.
The military rape,
It's done with drummers and a band.
You understand?
It's very grand!
It's done with drums and a great big brass band!

EL GALLO and FATHERS dance.

BELL: It's so Spanish; that's why I like it!
HUCK: I like it, too. Ai, yi, yi!

EL G: Just try to see it.
BELL: I see it!
HUCK: I see it!
EL G: And you will soon sí, sí, Señor.
Why—invite regret,
When you can get the sort of rape
You'll never ever forget!

FATHERS: We can get the rape
emphatic.
We can get the rape
polite.
We can get the rape
with Indians:
A truly charming sight.
We can get the rape on
horseback,
They all say it's new
and gay.
So you see the sort of
rape
Depends on what you
pay.
So you see the sort of
rape
Depends on what you
pay.

EL G: Oh, rape!
Sweet rape.
Oh, rape.
Ah—rape——
RA—AA—
AA—AA—
AA—PE!

ALL THREE:
Depends a lot
On what you—
HUCK: *Speaks.*
I say they're only young once—
Let's order us a First Class!

Left to right: WILLIAM LARSEN as Hucklebee, JE
ORBACH as El Gallo, HUGH THOMAS as Bellomy, ori
Sullivan Street produc

ALL THREE: *Sing.*
    Ra-aa-aa-pe!
    Olé!
EL G: *With pad and pencil.*
    One Rape First Class.
BELL: With trimmings!
EL G: *Makes note.*
    With trimmings. Now, let's see—is it to be a big
    affair, or intimate?
BELL: We thought—just the children.
EL G: I mean afterwards, at the party.
BELL: No. Just the immediate family.
EL G: No guests? Perhaps a gathering on the lawn?
BELL: Too expensive. Just the immediate family will be
    enough.
EL G: As you wish. That means the orchestra can go home.
    Still, big affairs are nice.
HUCK: Perhaps some other time.
EL G: All right then. You'd better go home and rehearse
    your parts.
    Exit FATHERS.

    La. Time is rushing. And a major production to do.
    I need actors—extra actors—to stage my elaborate
    Rape. But I'm not worried. Something will turn up.
    I can sense it in the air.
    Drumbeat.
    There—you hear? What did I tell you?

    *The MUTE opens the prop box and MORTIMER
    emerges, dressed in a loin cloth and a feather, and
    playing a drum. HE is followed at once by HENRY,
    an ancient actor down on his luck.*

HENRY: Sir, the Players have arrived!

EL G: Señor, the Players are most welcome.

HENRY: Don't look at us like we are, sir. Please. Remove
ten pounds of road dust from these aged wrinkled
cheeks. See make-up caked, in glowing powder pink!
Imagine a beard, full blown and blowing, like the
whiskers of a bear! And hair! Imagine hair. In a
box I've got all colors, so I beg you—imagine hair!
—And not these clothes. Oh no, no, no. Dear God,
not rags like any beggar has. But see me in a doublet!
Mortimer, fetch the doublet.

OMAS BRUCE (stage name for author TOM JONES) as
ary in the original Sullivan Street production.

N POMES as Mortimer, Sullivan Street.

MORTIMER sheathes him in a worn-out doublet.

There—Imagine! It's torn; I know—forget it. It
vanishes under light. That's it! That's the whole
trick; try to see me under light! I recite. Say a cue.
You'll see. I'll know it. Go on. Say one. Try me.

EL G: "Friends, Romans, Countrymen."
HENRY: It's what?
EL G: "Friends, Romans, Countrymen."
HENRY: —Don't tell me. I can get it. Let's see. "Friends,
Romans, Countrymen."

MORTIMER whispers it to him.

Why yes! Of course! That's easy. Why didn't you
pick something hard?

Strikes a pose.

Friends, Romans, Countrymen—
Screw your courage to the sticking place!
And be not sick and pale with grief
That thou—her handmaidens—
Should be far more fair
Than she . . . is . . .
How's that?

EL G: Amazing.
HENRY: Try to see it under light. I assure you it's dazzling.
I'm Henry Albertson. Perhaps you recall my
Hamlet?

EL G: Of course.
HENRY: *Stunned.*
You remember? Would you like to see the clippings?

EL G: Perhaps later.

HENRY: As you wish. I preserve them. Who knows—I may write a book someday. This is Mortimer; he does death scenes. He's been with me for forty years. Want to see one? He's an expert. Mortimer, die for the man.

MORTIMER dies.

You see! What did I tell you!—Now, down to business. You need Players?

EL G: For a love scene. Have you done romantic drama?

HENRY: That sir, is my specialty. Have you never seen my Romeo?

EL G: I'm afraid not.

HENRY: Oh well, I have the clippings.

Starts to get them, but EL GALLO grabs him.

EL G: Henry, here's the path: We'll have these players play something like the abduction of the maiden before this lover—

HENRY: *Catching the spirit.*
And if he but blench!

RICHARD CHAMBERLAIN, left, as El Gallo with JOHN CARRADINE as Henry. Arlington Park Theatre, Chicago.

EL G: We'll stand our ground. And fight until the lot of us
           is downed!
HENRY: Nobly done!
MORT: *Rising from the dead, and speaking with a very thick
           Cockney accent.*
           Where do you want me, 'Enry?
HENRY: Hm? Oh! Off left, Mortimer. Indians are always
           off left.
MORT: Wot's my cue?
HENRY: I'll tell you when it's time.
MORT: Righto.

           And HE exits—off stage left.

HENRY: *Calling out after him.*
           Don't forget, Mortimer: dress the stage, dress the
           stage. Don't cluster up when you die.

           To EL GALLO.

           Well, that does it, I think. I imagine we'd better
           hide.
EL G: Oh, I nearly forgot. I promised them moonlight.

           *HE snaps his fingers and the MUTE hangs up the
           moon.*

HENRY: Amazing!
EL G: Beautiful, eh? A lover's moon—
           Go ahead, Henry. I'll be right there.

           *HENRY exits, and EL GALLO speaks to the audi-
           ence as the MUTE mimes the sensations and the
           words.*

You wonder how these things begin.
Well, this begins with a glen.
It begins with a Season, which,
For want of a better word,
We might as well call September.

MUSIC.

It begins with a forest where the woodchucks woo
And leaves wax green,
And vines entwine like lovers; try to see it:
Not with your eyes, for they are wise;
But see it with your ears:
The cool green breathing of the leaves.
And hear it with the inside of your hand:
The soundless sound of shadows flicking light.
Celebrate sensation.
Recall that secret place;
You've been there, you remember:
That special place where once—
Just once—in your crowded sunlit lifetime,
You hid away in shadows from the tyranny of time.
That spot beside the clover
Where someone's hand held your hand,
And love was sweeter than the berries,
Or the honey,
Or the stinging taste of mint.
It is September,
Before a rainfall—
A perfect time to be in love.

Enter MATT and LUISA.

MATT: Hello.

LUISA: Hello.
My father is going to be very angry.
MATT: I know. So is mine.
LUISA: We've never been here at night.
MATT: No.
LUISA: It's different from the day.
MATT: Are you frightened?
LUISA: Yes; no.
Brr. It's cold here. There's going to be a storm.
MATT: Would you like my jacket?
LUISA: No, thank you. Matt.
MATT: Yes?
LUISA: My hand is trembling.
MATT: Don't be afraid. Please.
LUISA: All right. I promise.

Thunder. LUISA rushes into MATT's arms.

MATT: There, there. It's all right.
LUISA: Matt, take care of me. Teach me. I don't want to be awkward—or afraid. I love you, Matt. I want there to be a happy ending.
MATT: I promise that there will be.
Kisses her.
Look.
LUISA: What?
MATT: *Smiles.*
My hand is trembling too.

LUISA: *Sings.*
Hear how the wind begins to whisper.
See how the leaves go streaming by.
Smell how the velvet rain is falling,
Out where the fields are warm and dry.

LIZA MINELLI as Luisa in the
Westport Country Playhouse
production co-starring ELLIOTT
GOULD as El Gallo.

Now is the time to run inside and stay.
Now is the time to find a hideaway—
Where we can stay.

MATT: Soon it's gonna rain;
I can see it.
Soon it's gonna rain;
I can tell.
Soon it's gonna rain;
What are we gonna do?

Soon it's gonna rain;
I can feel it.
Soon it's gonna rain;
I can tell.
Soon it's gonna rain;
What'll we do with you?

We'll find four limbs of a tree.
We'll build four walls and a floor.
We'll bind it over with leaves.
Then duck inside to stay.

Then we'll let it rain;
We'll not feel it.
Then we'll let it rain;
Rain pell-mell.
And we'll not complain
If it never stops at all.
We'll live and love
Within our own four walls.

THEY talk now, as the MUSIC continues.

Would you like for me to show you around the
castle?

LUISA: Oh yes, please.

MATT: The lookout tower. And the throne. And this, the family pride and joy: the ballroom!

LUISA: My, how grand.

MATT: Princess.

LUISA: Your highness.

And THEY begin to dance—at first grand and sweeping and then more and more tenderly as the wind continues to swirl in. As the thunder rolls again, MATT pulls her up on the platform and the MUTE sprinkles them with paper rain.

MATT: We'll find four limbs of a tree.
We'll build four walls and a floor.
We'll bind it over with leaves,
Then duck inside to stay.

BOTH: Then we'll let it rain;
We'll not feel it.
Then we'll let it rain;
Rain pell-mell.
And we'll not complain
If it never stops at all.
We'll live and love
Within our castle walls.

At the end of the song, HENRY comes back in. HE signals for the Audience to be quiet; then HE speaks to the MUSICIANS.

HENRY: Accelerando con molto!

As the MUSIC begins for the Rape Ballet, HENRY calls out "Swords" to the MUTE, who

*rushes to the prop box and removes four wooden
sticks. Then HENRY calls out:*

Indians, ready?
Indians—Rape!

*And MORTIMER springs out of his hiding place.
HE snatches up the astonished LUISA right before
the eyes of the equally astonished MATT and starts
to carry her out Right. But HENRY, in a fury, in-
terrupts him.*

Left to right: THOMAS BRUCE
as Henry, KENNETH NELSON as Matt,
and RITA GARDNER as Luisa,
original Sullivan Street production.

HENRY: No, no. Off Left, Damn it!
MORT: All right, all right.

And HE faithfully totes her left. By now MATT has recovered himself sufficiently to interrupt their progress. HE struggles with MORTIMER as HENRY grabs up the disentangled LUISA. MOR-TIMER rushes over. HE and HENRY pick up the girl and try to carry her out—each in a different direction, of course. The MUTE hands MATT the drum sticks to MORTIMER's Indian Drum, and MATT floors both the old actors with a mighty whop of the sticks. LUISA rushes up to her pro-tector as HENRY struggles to his feet.

HENRY: *Feeling his head.*
"A touch, A touch. I do confess it."

Now, the moment is ripe for the big scene. HENRY rushes to the side and yells out: "Cavalry!" which is the cue for EL GALLO to enter into the fray. EL GALLO sweeps on with a flourish. The MUTE supplies both HE and MATT with wood swords and THEY begin to fight. During the midst of their battle, EL GALLO is thrown to the side and HENRY catches him and yells out: "Once more, dear friends, into the breach!" At this signal the MUTE supplies HENRY and MORTIMER with stick swords and all three "villains" sword-fight our young hero at once—not at all unlike the Douglas Fairbanks movies of the good old days. THEY advance. THEY retreat. Then—with a mighty push, MATT sends them all sprawling to the floor. MORTIMER rises—rushes forward—

is killed dramatically. HENRY rises—and as HE charges, cries out—

HENRY: "God for Harry, England, and Saint Geo - - ough!"

The last word becomes a vivid "ouch" as HE is wounded and falls dead. Only EL GALLO is left now. HE and MATT square off and have at it. For a while it's nip and tuck as the two men fight up and down upon the platform, and clash together every once in a while so that THEY stand gritting, tooth to tooth, across the criss-crossed sabers. In the end, EL GALLO allows himself to be defeated and HE dies in so grand a manner that even MORTIMER cannot resist a look of admiration. EL GALLO dies like a diva in the opera, rising again and again from the floor, to give one last dramatic, agonized twitch.

When EL GALLO goes down for the last time, the MUSIC becomes jolly and triumphant. The young lovers rush upon the little platform and embrace in a pretty tableau. The FATHERS rush in too. And embrace too. And get upon the platform to finish off the "Living Statues" type of tableau.

All these speeches are over MUSIC.

LUISA: Matt!
MATT: Luisa!
HUCK: Son!
BELL: Daughter!
HUCK: *To BELL.*
Neighbor!

48

BELL: *To HUCK.*
Friend!
LUISA: *To the world.*
I always knew there would be a happy ending!

*The MUSIC suddenly stops. THEY all freeze as
EL GALLO rises, rather painfully, from the dead.*

EL G: *Feeling his back.*
I think I pulled something.

MORT: Oh, you get a bit sore at first; dying like that. It's not the easiest thing in the business. But I like it. I've been dying for forty years, ever since I was a boy. Ah, you should have seen me in those days. I could die off a twenty foot cliff backwards! People used to cry out: "Die again, Mortimer—die again!" But of course I never did.

EL G: Well, Henry. Are you off now?

HENRY: Yes. Going somewhere. There's not much left to the old Company anymore—just Mortimer and me. But we make out. I recite Shakespeare. Mortimer dies. There's usually an audience somewhere. Oh—here's your moon.

EL G: Thank you—"Good night, Sweet Prince."

HENRY: *After first pushing MORTIMER out of "his" light.* "And flights of angels sing thee to thy rest—Why doth the drum come hither?" Remember, Mortimer, there are no small actors—only small parts.

HENRY and MORTIMER step back into the prop box, and—just before HE disappears under the lid, HENRY looks out to the audience and speaks.

Remember me—in light!

Drawing by HARVEY SCHMIDT
of original cast in first act tableau.

And HE is gone. EL GALLO looks at the
LOVERS and their PARENTS still frozen on the
stage. Like a choral conductor, HE conducts them
in the short contrapuntal selection called "HAPPY
ENDING"

EL G: *When THEY are through singing.*
Very pretty, eh?
Worthy of Watteau.
A group of living statues:
What do they call it?
A tableau.
Hmmm.
I wonder if they can hold it.
They'll try to, I suppose.
And yet it won't be easy
To hold such a pretty pose.
We'll see.
We'll leave them for a little
Then we'll see.

EL GALLO and the MUTE hang the "FAN-
TASTICKS" drape, in front of the actors.

Act One is over.
It's the Intermission now.

51

Act II

KEITH CHARLES as El Gallo, Sullivan Street production.

EL GALLO *re-enters, carrying the moon. HE nods to the MUTE, who undoes the flap and lowers the curtain on the little platform stage. The PARENTS and the LOVERS are still there, poised in their pretty tableau. But THEY seem less graceful now, as if there were some pain involved in holding the pose so long.*

EL G: Their moon was cardboard, fragile.
It was very apt to fray,
And what was last night scenic
May seem cynic by today.
The play's not done.
Oh no—not quite,
For life never ends in the moonlit night;
And despite what pretty poets say,
The night is only half the day.

So we would like to truly finish
What was foolishly begun.
For the story is not ended
And the play is never done
Until we've all of us been burned a bit
And burnished by—the sun!

 HE reverses the moon. On the other side is the sun. HE throws it into the air, making daylight. And one by one, the PARENTS and the CHILDREN begin to break from the tableau. Their eyes sting in the hot red sun. The music underneath is sour—disgruntled.

HUCK: It's hot.
BELL: What?
HUCK: Hot!

BELL: Oh. Sssss—
LUISA: And now we can meet in the sunlight.
MATT: And now there is no more wall.
LUISA: Aren't we happy?
MATT: Yes. Aren't we.

Chord.

LUISA: He looks different in the sunlight.
MATT: I'm not ready to get married yet.
LUISA: I thought he was taller, somehow.
MATT: When you get right down to it, she's only the girl
next door.

Chord.

HUCK: Neighbor.
BELL: Friend.
HUCK: In-law.

BELL: Ugh.

Chord.

HUCK: This is what we've always wanted.
Our gardens are one.
BELL: We're merged.
HUCK: Related.
BELL: Amalga-
HUCK: Mated.
BELL: Well.

*Chord! As MATT and LUISA step down off the
platform, HUCK gets his clippers and BELL his
watering pail.*

LUISA: What shall we do today?
MATT: Whatever you say.

LUISA: And tomorrow?
MATT: The same!

Chord.

I wonder where that road goes.
LUISA: I'd like to swim in a clear blue stream—

Chord.

HUCK: Water, water, water!
BELL: What did you say?
HUCK: I said, Water, Water, Water!
BELL: Clip, Clip, Clip!
HUCK: What?
BELL: You're clipping my kumquat!
HUCK: Rot!

BERT LAHR as Hucklebee in the Hallmark Hall
of Fame television production.

*The music for the quartet has begun as the FOUR
PRINCIPALS pace back and forth, MATT and
LUISA eating plums which the MUTE has given
to them.*

LUISA: This plum is too ripe!
MATT: Sorry.

Music.

Please don't watch me while I'm eating.
LUISA: Sorry.

Music.

HUCK: You're about to drown that magnolia!
BELL: Sorry!

Music.

You're—standing—in—my—KUMQUAT!

HUCK: *SORRY!*

*And the quartet begins, first as solos, and then as a
round.*

LUISA: Take away the golden moonbeam.
Take away the tinsel sky.
What at night seems oh so scenic,
May be cynic by and by.

MATT: Take away the painted sunset.
Take away the blue lagoon.
What at night seems oh so scenic,
May be cynic much too soon.

BELL: Take away the secret meetings.
Take away the chance to fight.
What at night seems oh so scenic
May be cynic in the light.

HUCK: Take away the sense of drama.
Take away the puppet play.
What at night seems oh so scenic
May be cynic by today.

ALL: So take it away and paint it up right!
Yes, take it away and decorate it!
So take it away, that sun is too bright!
I say that it really is a pity;
It used to be so pretty.

And now the round, ending with:

MATT: *Spoken.*
This plum is too ripe!

ALL: SORRY!

HUCK: *When the music is over.*
I was a fool to tear down that wall.

BELL: So was I. I hate people tromping in my garden!

LUISA: Please. No fighting.
You see, I come like Cassandra
With a figleaf in my hand.

BELL: It was Minerva.

HUCK: And that's a plum.

LUISA: Well!

MATT: Don't mind them, dear.
I think they're jealous.

HUCK: Jealous?

MATT: Of us. Of our passion—and our youth.

59

BELL: Fantastic!
MATT: You see—they are jealous!
LUISA: It's sweet—just like drama.
 Fathers always play the fool.
HUCK: I could speak, if I chose to—
MATT: Speak what?
BELL: Shh. Better not.
HUCK: No. I'll be silent.
 But you'd better not push it much further.
MATT: You forget that I'm a hero.
 After all, there's my rapier—
LUISA: And my rape!
MATT: Ah, what swordplay! Now, that was really living!
LUISA: That handsome bandit—ah, what hands!
 He grabbed me—here!
 I've put a little ribbon on the spot.
MATT: Hot-blooded bandits!
 And I cut them down like wheat!
HUCK: I could speak, but I won't.
BELL: It's tempting, but we shouldn't.
LUISA: It should be made into an epic poem.
MATT: I'll write it.
LUISA: Or better yet—a shrine.
MATT: Divine! I'll build it.

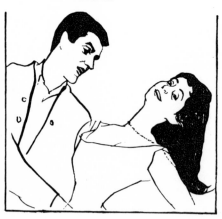

JACK BLACKTON as Matt and ROYCE LENELLE as Luisa, Sullivan Street
production, drawing by WILLIAM AUERBACH-LEVY.

LUISA: Where the wall was.
MATT: This very spot I heard your call,
And here beside our fathers' wall,
I drew my sword and slew them all,
How many—twenty?
LUISA: Thirty!
MATT: Yes!—Or even thirty-two.
And every one there was to slay,
I slew!

And LUISA swoons in his arms.

HUCK: Ass.
MATT: I beg your pardon?
HUCK: I say that you're an ass!
MATT: *Laughs.*
Charming!
LUISA: *Also laughing.*
Isn't it? He behaves like a pantaloon!
HUCK: By God, that does it!
BELL: Wait!
HUCK: No. I'm no pantaloon!
You think that walls come tumbling down?
You think that brigands find an open gate—
The way prepared—You think it's Fate?
MATT: What do you mean?
HUCK: You think that fathers play the fool
To children barely out of school?
LUISA: They do in books.
HUCK: In books, maybe.
It's not the same in reality.
No, children—
Children act on puppet stages

Prepared by parents' hard-won wages.
Or do you think such things can be?
You think a First Class Rape comes free!
By God, look at that; it's the villain's fee!

MATT: What is this?

BELL: An itemized bill for your pretty little Rape.

LUISA: But the feud?

HUCK: We arranged it.

MATT: And the wall?

BELL: Built to fall.

MATT: I don't believe it.

HUCK: Read on, Macduff!

MATT: *Reads,*
"Item—a silver piece for actor to portray Indian Raiding Party—body paint included."
"Item—a piece in gold to the famous El Gallo for allowing himself to seem wounded by a beardless, callow boy."
"Item—one moon—"

MATT looks up.

I see you spared no pains.

LUISA: You mean it wasn't real? The Bandit? The moon-light—?

MATT: Everything!

LUISA: But it isn't fair. We didn't need your moon, or bandits. We're in love! We could have made our own moons!

BELL: *Touched.*
My child.

MATT: We were just puppets!

LUISA: A marriage of convenience!

BELL: You see. You've spoiled everything!
HUCK: I told you it wouldn't work.
BELL: You told? *You?* Why, you liar.
Get out of my kumquat!
HUCK: Damn your kumquat!

And HE clips it down to the ground as BELL gasps in horror.

BELL: That does it! You're a murderer!
HUCK: And you're a fool.
BELL: Let go of my arm!
HUCK: Stop clipping my hat!

THEY struggle briefly.

BELL: By God, that does it! I'm going to build up my wall!
HUCK: I too!
BELL: I'll lime mine up with bottles!

HUCK: I'll jag mine up with glass!
EL G: *Comes center to break up the fight.*
Pardon me.
FATHERS: Damn!

And THEY exit.

MATT: *Springs up.*
Wait!
LUISA: Oh look! It's my bandit.
MATT: You are—
Looks at the bill.
El Gallo?

Original costume design for JERRY ORBACH as
El Gallo by ED WITTSTEIN.

EL G: Sometimes.

MATT: About this bill. I think you earned it rather easily.

EL G: You made it easy to earn.

MATT: That's true. But now I will make it harder. Where is my sword! Somebody get me a sword!

EL G: Nice boy.

The MUTE hands MATT a sword.

MATT: En garde!

EL G: Up a bit with the wrist.
That foot back more.
Aim at the entrails.
That's good—encore!
Thrust One—Thrust Two;
Bend the knee—Thrust Three!
But then be sure to parry—
Like this, see.

HE disarms MATT and throws the sword back to the MUTE.

Another lesson?

MATT: God, I'm a fool!

LUISA: Always bragging.

MATT: Don't be sarcastic.

LUISA: I shall be sarcastic whenever I choose.

MATT: You think I couldn't do it?

LUISA: I think you'd better grow up.

MATT: Grow up! Grow up!
And this from a girl who is sixteen!

LUISA: Girls mature faster.

MATT: No. This can't be happening.
If I'm not mad,
If I'm not gloriously insane,

Helsinki, Finland, Municipal Theatre production:
ANJA HAAHDENMAA as Luisa, STIG FRANSMAN as Matt.

	Then I'm just me again.
	And if I'm me—
	Then I can see.
LUISA:	What?
MATT:	Everything. All the flaws.
	You're childish.
LUISA:	Child-like.
MATT:	Silly.
LUISA:	Soulful.
MATT:	And you have freckles!
LUISA:	*Suddenly outraged.*
	That's a lie!
MATT:	I can see them under those pounds of powder. Look.
	Freckles!
LUISA:	I hate you.
MATT:	You see: self-deception. It's a sign of immaturity to
	wear lavender perfume before you're forty.
LUISA:	You're a poseur. I've heard you talking in the garden,
	walking around reciting romantic poems about your-
	self. Ha—the bold hero.
MATT:	You're adolescent.
LUISA:	Ahh!

And SHE slaps him. There is a pause. Then as THEY speak, their anger is underscored by music.

MATT:	Beyond that road lies adventure.
LUISA:	I'm going to take my hair down and go swimming in the stream.
MATT:	You'll never hear of me again, my dear. I've decided to be bad.
LUISA:	I'll sit up all night and sing songs to the moon.
MATT:	I'll drink and gamble! I'll grow a moustache.
	I'll find my madness—somewhere, out there.

LUISA: I'll find mine too. I'll have an affair!
MATT: Goodbye forever!
LUISA: See if I care!

THEY start to leave. EL GALLO snaps his fingers, and THEY stop, frozen in their tracks. EL GALLO takes tear from LUISA's face.

EL G: This tear is enough—this tiny tear.
HE carefully puts it in his pocket..
A boy may go;

The girl must stay.
Thus runs the world away.

Exit LUISA

MATT is still frozen front, caught in the middle of a dream.

See, he sees it.
And the world seems very grand.

The music has begun, and now MATT sings, as EL GALLO echoes him cynically.

MATT: Beyond that road lies a shining world.
EL G: Beyond that road lies despair.
MATT: Beyond that road lies a world that's gleaming—
EL G: People who are scheming.
MATT: Beauty!
EL G: Hunger.
MATT: Glory!
EL G: Sorrow.
MATT: Never a pain or care.
EL G: He's liable to find a couple of surprises there.

Now EL GALLO sings and Matt echoes.

ARMANDO CALVO as El Gallo,
Mexico City production,
drawing by PACO RIVERO GIL.

KENNETH NELSON as Matt,
original Sullivan Street production.

There's a song he must sing;
It's a well-known song
But the tune is bitter
And it doesn't take long to learn.
MATT: I can learn!
EL G: That pretty little world that beams so bright.
       That pretty little world that seems delightful
       can burn!
MATT: Let me learn!
       Let me learn!

reality therapy

*And as the tempo picks up, MATT sings of his
vision..*

For I can see it!
Shining somewhere!
Bright lights somewhere invite me to come there
And learn!
And I'm ready!

I can hear it!
Sirens singing!
Inside my ear I hear them all singing:
Come learn!

Who knows—maybe—
All the visions that I see
May be waiting just for me

To say—take me there, and
Make me see it!
Make me feel it!
I know it's so, I know that it really
May be!
Let me learn!

	I can see it!
EL G:	He can see it.
MATT:	Shining somewhere!
EL G:	Shining somewhere.
	Those lights not only glitter, but once there—
	They burn!

MATT:	I can hear it!
EL G:	He can hear it.
MATT:	Sirens singing!
EL G:	Sirens singing.
	Don't listen close or maybe you'll never
	Return!

BOTH:	Who knows—may be—
	All the visions he (I) can see—
	May be waiting just for me
	To say—take me there—and

MATT:	Make me see those shining sights inside of me!
EL G:	Make him see it!
MATT:	Make me feel those lights inside don't lie to me!
EL G:	Make him feel it!

MATT:	I know it's so, I know that it really
	May be.
	This is what I've always waited for!
	This is what my life's created for!
BOTH:	Let me (him) learn!
EL G:	*Speaks when the music is over.*
	The world will teach him
	Very quickly
	The secret he needs to know.
	A certain parable about Romance;

And so—we let him go.
We commit him to the tender mercies
Of that most stringent teacher—Time.
But just so there's no slip-up
We'll add a bit—of spice.

*Enter MORTIMER and HENRY from Prop Box
in stringy wigs and once-colorful disguises.*

BLACK
Pirates Hat
OR
BANDANA
_____
BALLOON
TA FFETTA
Pantaloons
_____
Bolero
_____
BELT
_____
ankle Bracelet
_____
PAGE.

Mortimer
ACT II
PIRATE
"The Fantastiks"

Signature

Act two costume for Mortimer :
original designs by ED WITTSTEIN.

MORT: Hold on there a minute, Matie!
MATT: What?
HENRY: And where may you be going, my fiery-eyed young
        friend? Don't answer; I can see it in your eyes.
MORT: I see it too—them beady eyes!
HENRY: You go for the goose—the golden goose that lays the
        platinum-plated egg, right? Right! I am Lodevigo
        —just like yourself—a young man looking for the
        pleasánt pinch of adventure.
MATT: Young man!
HENRY: Yes! And to your left, observe this seamy individual;
        he is my companion who goes by the name of—
        Socrates.
MORT: I'm Roman.
HENRY: Romanoff, he means. A blue-blood.
        He is descended from the Tzars.
MATT: The Tzars?
HENRY: He is, in fact, the noblest Romanoff of them all.
        But enough of chit-chat.
MORT: Enough. Enough.
HENRY: You long for adventure? We will take you, won't
        we, Socci?
MORT: We'll take him, all right!
HENRY: To the places you've dreamed of—
        Venice—Egypt! Ah—Egypt—
        "I am dying, Egypt!"—that's a line from some-
        thing. I don't recall just what.
MATT: I thought I would—
HENRY: Seek your fortune! Exactly why we're here.
        Right, Socci?
MORT: Right, Loddi. We're going to give you the works!
HENRY: The fireworks, he means.

EDWARD EVERETT HORTON as Henry
in the John Kenley Theatres production,
drawing by GROSS.

MATT: It was my intention—
HENRY: Forget intentions! They paved the road to hell.
We'll see to your education.
MORT: We know all the ropes!
HENRY: And the ropes to skip, as well!
MORT: 'Eathen idols!
HENRY: Whirling girlies!
MORT: Tipsy gypsies!
HENRY: Fantastic beauty—just waiting to be unzipped!
MATT: But I—
HENRY: *Clapping his hand over MATT's mouth,*
Don't bother to thank us!
MORT: *Doing likewise,*
Right! Let's hurry! Loddi—Hurry!
BOTH: *Singing as THEY up-end him,*

Beyond that road—
Is an Episode—
An episode—
An episode—
Beyond that road is an episode—
Look out, you nearly tripped!
Hip. Hip.
Beyond that road is an episode,
An Episode, an episode—
Beyond that road is an episode—
Just waiting to be unzipped!
Hey!

THEY exit carrying MATT.

EL G: Now grant me in your minds a month.
October is over and the sky grows gray.
A month goes by,

71

It's a little bit colder.
A month goes by
We're one month older.

Enter BELLOMY wearing his winter scarf.

BELL: *To MUTE, who is building wall.*
That's fine. There's nothing better than a good thick wall. Keep working, friend. Keep working!

HE exits, and HUCKLEBEE comes in on his side. HE sports a winter scarf.

HUCK: Still progressing? Good. We want to get it finished before snowfall.

HE exits, and BELLOMY returns.

BELL: Hmmm. Getting colder. I'll just take a look at the wall. Fine! Keep on working—Lord, this weather makes a man feel old.

Exit. Enter HUCKLEBEE.

HUCK: Not a word. He's been gone for a month, and I haven't had a single word.

To the MUTE.

How's it going? Hmmm? Oh, I forgot. You're not supposed to talk.

HUCKLEBEE sits in his garden as BELLOMY reappears.

BELL: Luisa?—Now dear, listen. It's silly to stand in the garden. You'll catch pneumonia. You'll catch asthma. Luisa?
No response.
Well, anyway—I brought you a little shawl.

Odense, Denmark, Odense Teater production: HOLGER PERFORT as Bellomy, GITTE HAENNING as Luisa.

*The FATHERS see each other. THEY hesitate,
and then bow gravely. Then THEY stand, face to
face, watching the MUTE at work.*

BELL: *To the MUTE.*
       I don't suppose you'd care to see my garden?

HUCK: He won't answer.

BELL: I don't recall addressing that remark to you, sir.

HUCK: He's not supposed to speak.

BELL: Oh— Oh, well. —By the way . . .

HUCK: *Eagerly.*
       Yes?

BELL: Oh—nothing.
       HUCKLEBEE begins to chuckle.
       What's so funny?

HUCK: I was just thinking how we used to meet.

BELL: *Smiles.*
       Climbing over the wall.

HUCK: Secret meetings—

BELL: Just to play a little game of cards.
       THEY both laugh in delight.
       Becoming serious.
       How's your son?

HUCK: Not a word.

BELL:	He'll come back— When he runs out of your money.
HUCK:	Thank you. And your daughter?
BELL:	Like a statue. Does nothing but dream all day.
HUCK:	Pity. —How's your garden?
BELL:	Growing!
HUCK:	Mine too.
BELL:	So dependable.
	Gardens go on growing.
HUCK:	Yes indeed, they do.
BELL:	I tell you, I love vegetables.
HUCK:	It's true. I love them too.

And THEY shake hands and sing.

Plant a radish;
Get a radish.
Never any doubt
That's why I love vegetables;
You know what you're about!

Plant a turnip; get a turnip.
Maybe you'll get two.
That's why I love vegetables;
You know that they'll come through!

They're dependable!
They're befriendable!
They're the best pal a parent's ever known!
While with children—
It's bewilderin'
You don't know until the seed is nearly grown,
Just what you've sown.

So
Plant a carrot,

DONALD BABCOCK
(above) as Hucklebee and
JOHN MARTIN as Bellomy,
Sullivan Street production.

Get a carrot,
Not a brussel sprout.
That's why I love vegetables,
You know what you're about!

Life is merry,
If it's very
Vegitari—an.
A man who plants a garden
Is a very happy man!

*This second chorus THEY sing like a vaudeville
team, complete with little awkward dance steps.*

Plant a beanstalk;
Get a beanstalk.
Just the same as Jack.
Then if you don't like it,
You can always take it back!

But if your issue
Doesn't kiss you,
Then I wish you luck.
For once you've planted children,
You're absolutely stuck!

Every turnip green!
Every kidney bean!
Every plant grows according to the plot!
While with progeny,
It's hodge-podgenee,
For as soon as you think you know what kind you've
    got,
It's what they're not!

75

So
Plant a cabbage;
Get a cabbage;
Not a sauerkraut!
That's why I love vegetables,
You know what you're about!

Life is merry
If it's very
Vegitari—an.
A man who plants a garden
Is a very happy man!

He's a vegitari—
Very merry
Vegitari—an!

BELL: *When the song is over.*
Say, what about that game of pinochle?
HUCK: I prefer poker.
BELL: All right, but let's hurry!
HUCK: You still owe me from last time.
To the MUTE.
You keep on working.
BELL: He's a nice chap.

THEY exit.

LUISA, meanwhile, has begun to come out of her trance.

LUISA: Oh! Oh! Oh!
Sings,
I'd like to swim in a clear blue stream
Where the water is icy cold.

        Then go to town in a golden gown
        And have my fortune told.

EL G: *Sings.*
        Just once!
        Just once!
        Just once before you're old!

LUISA: It's my bandit!
EL G: Your bandit, yes.
LUISA: What are you doing up in that tree?
EL G: Growing ripe.
LUISA: Don't grow too ripe or you'll fall.
EL G: Very wise.

LUISA:	What do you see from up there?
EL G:	Everything.
LUISA:	Really?
EL G:	Nearly.
LUISA:	Do you see Matt?
EL G:	Do you care?
LUISA:	No, I just wondered.
	Can I climb up there beside you?
EL G:	You can if you can.
LUISA:	*Joins him,*
	There!
	I don't see everything.
EL G:	It takes a little while.
LUISA:	All I see is my own house. And Matt's.
	And the wall.
EL G:	And that's all?
LUISA:	All.
	Is it fun to be a bandit?
EL G:	It has its moments.
LUISA:	I think it must be fun.
	Tell me,
	Do you ride on a great white horse?
EL G:	I used to.
LUISA:	But no longer?
EL G:	I developed a saddle rash.
	Very painful.
LUISA:	How unglamorous.
	I never heard of a hero
	Who had a saddle rash.
EL G:	Oh, it happens. Occupational hazard.
LUISA:	Tell me,
	What is your favourite plunder?

EL G: Plunder?
          I think that's Pirates.
LUISA: Well then, booty.
EL G: You've been reading too many books.
LUISA: Well, you must steal *something!*
EL G: I steal fancies. I steal whatever is treasured most.
LUISA: That's more like it—
          Precious rubies!

EL G: *Looking at her necklace.*
          Precious rhinestones.
LUISA: Rhinestones?
EL G: Can be precious.
          It depends on the point of view.
LUISA: Well, it doesn't sound very sound.
          Economically, I mean.
EL G: Pretty child.
LUISA: Do you think so?
          Do I attract you?
EL G: Somewhat.
LUISA: Oh, that's splendid!
          Look, see this ribbon.
          That's where you gave me a bruise.
EL G: I'm so sorry.
LUISA: Don't be silly. I adore it!
          I kiss it three times every day.
          Tell me,
          Have you seen the world?
EL G: A bit, yes.
LUISA: Is it like in the books?
EL G: Depends on which books you read.
LUISA: The adventures. The Romances.

	"Cast off thy name.
	A rose by any other name—"
	Do you know that?
EL G:	Sounds familiar.
LUISA:	"Put up thy sword. The dew will rust it!"
	That's Othello. He was older than Desdemona,
	But she loved him because he had seen the world.
	Of course he killed her.
EL G:	Of course.
LUISA:	"It's a far better thing that I do now
	Than I have ever done before!"
	Isn't that beautiful? That man was beheaded.
EL G:	I'm not surprised.
LUISA:	Take me there!
EL G:	Where?
LUISA:	To the parties! To the world!
EL G:	But I'm a bandit.
	There is a price upon my head.
LUISA:	Oh. I was hoping that there would be!
EL G:	You and I!
	Us together!

London production: TERENCE COOPER as El Gallo, STEPHANIE VOSS as Luisa.

LUISA: Yes. Dancing forever and forever!
EL G: *Sings.*

Round and round
Till the break of day.
Candles glow,
Fiddles play,
Why not be wild if we feel that way?
Reckless and terribly gay!

Round and round,
'Neath a magic spell.
Velvet gown,
Pink lapel.
Life is a colorful carousel.
Reckless and terribly gay!

LUISA: I'm ready anytime.
If you'll take me, I'm
Ready to go!
So show the way to me,
I will try to be,
Ready to go!

EL G: I seem to see Venice,
We're on a lagoon.
A gondolier's crooning
A gondola tune.
The air makes your hair billow blue in the moon.
LUISA: I could swoon!
EL G: You're so blue in the moon!

*And now THEY begin to dance. The MUTE
hands her a mask—a paper mask of a blank face; a
laughing-hollow mask; a stylish face that is frozen*

forever into unutterable joy. This mask is upon a little hand-stick—so that when held in front of one's visage, it blocks out any little tell-tale traces of compassion or of horror.

As LUISA and EL GALLO go on dancing, we see —in a stylized blaze of light—MORTIMER and HENRY up on the platform stage—waving "flames" of torn red silk. At first THEY are gondoliers—but as the action gets wilder, THEY change into rioting peasants. In each of these sequences, it is MATT who is the object of their fury

Left to right: TOM LACY as Mortimer, CAROLE DEMAS as Luisa, JOE BELLOMO as El Gallo, and F. MURRAY ABRAHAM as Henry, Sullivan Street production.

LUISA: *Spoken.*
Look at the peasants.
They're lighting candelabras.
No, I believe they're lighting torches.
Yes, see—
They've started burning the palaces.
—There goes the Doge!
HENRY: A rivederci!
LUISA: Oh, what fun!
I *adore* pyrotechnics!

Suddenly MORTIMER and HENRY set MATT
on fire.

LUISA: That man—look out; he's burning.
My God, he's on fire!
EL G: Keep on dancing.
LUISA: But he's burning—
EL G: Just put up your mask—
Then it's pretty.
MATT: Help! Help!

EL GALLO raises the mask to her face.

LUISA: Oh yes, isn't he *beautiful!*
He's all sort of orange.
Red-orange.
That's one of my favorite colors!
MATT: Help!
LUISA: You look lovely!

MORTIMER and HENRY pull MATT down
and out of sight as the MUTE holds up a silk cloth
to shield them—the effect being rather like a Punch
and Judy show that is being performed on the plat-
form.

EL G: *As LUISA sings a wild obligato.*
We'll just
Dance!
We'll kick up our heels to music
And dance!
Until my head reels with music
Like a lovely real romance,
All we'll do is daily dance.
All we'll do is just dance.
All we'll do is just dance.
All we'll do is just—

LUISA: *Speaks.*
Whee. I'm exhausted.

EL G: *Speaks.*
But you can't be.
The evening's just started!

MUSIC. As HE starts singing again.

Round and round
Till the break of day.
Candles glow.
Fiddles play.
Why not be wild if we feel that way.
Reckless and terribly gay!

LUISA: I'm ready anytime,
If you'll take me, I'm
Ready to go!
So show the way to me,
I will try to be,
Ready to go!

EL G: I seem to see Athens, it's terribly chic.
Atop the Acropolis, it's terribly Greek.
There's Venus, Adonis, 'n us—cheek to cheek.
LUISA: Oh how chic!
EL G: To be Greek cheek to cheek!

*Once more we see MORTIMER and HENRY in
colorful attire. And once more MATT is along with
them. HE is ragged and disheveled—and HE is
much the worse for wear.*

LUISA: *Speaks.*
Observe the friendly natives!
La, how gay.
Look dear, they're beating a monkey.
Isn't that fun.
I wonder why anyone should be beating a monkey?
Oh no, that's it.
It's not a monkey at all.
It's a man dressed in a monkey suit.
That man—they've hurt him!
EL G: Put up the mask.
LUISA: But he is wounded.
EL G: The Mask! The Mask!
MATT: Help!

*And once more EL GALLO presses the sophisti-
cated mask up to her face.*

LUISA: Oh, isn't that cute.
They're beating a man in a monkey suit.
It's a show. La, how jolly.
Don't stop; it's charming.
Don't stop.

MATT: Help!
LUISA: That's it. Writhe some more.

And the "puppets" disappear again, as the MUTE holds up the cloth in front of them.

EL G: We'll just
Dance!
We'll kick up our heels to music
And dance!
Until my head reels with music
Like a lovely real romance.
All we'll do is daily dance.
All we'll do is just dance.
All we'll do is just dance.
All we'll do is just—

LUISA: *Speaks.*
Couldn't we just sit this one out?
EL G: *Speaks.*
Ridiculous! When there's music to be danced to?
Play gypsies!

JOHN CUNNINGHAM as
El Gallo and ROYCE LENELLE
as Luisa, Sullivan Street
production.

BOTH: Round and round
'Neath a magic spell.
Velvet gown,
Pink lapel.
Life is a colorful carousel.
Reckless and terribly gay.

LUISA: I'm ready anytime.
If you'll take me, I'm
Ready to go!
So show the way to me,
I will try to be,
Ready to go!

EL G: We'll be in Bengazi or maybe Bombay.
I understand Indja is terribly gay.
The natives assemble on feast day and play

LUISA: With their snakes?

EL G: What a racket it makes!

LUISA: *Speaks.*
I think I'm going to love Indja.
Such a big population, and
I adore crowds!
Oh look, there's a fakir—
Hi, Fakir!

HENRY: *A bit confused.*
A rivederci!

LUISA: See—he's there with his assistants.
They all know Yogi—
And they're just loads of fun!
There's one—a young one—
They're putting him down on some nails.
SHE puts down her mask.

	If he fails,
	He'll be cut to bits by those nails.
MATT:	Help!
LUISA:	Someone help him.
EL G:	The mask!
LUISA:	But he's bleeding!
EL G:	Mask!
LUISA:	Horrible!
EL G:	Mask!

And HE forces it up to her face. Once more, the transition.

LUISA:	Go on. Sit down harder.
	He's a sissy.
	I don't believe he's a real fakir.
	They never complain.
	He's a fake fakir.
MATT:	Help!
LUISA:	Fake!
ALL:	*Sing.*
	We'll—
	Just—
	Dance—!
	We'll kick up our heels to music
	And dance!
	Until my head reels with music.
	Like a lovely real romance,
	All we'll do is daily
	I can see the friendly natives!
	All we'll do is just dance.
	All we'll do is just dance.
	All we'll do is just—

88

Round and round in a magic spell.
All we'll do is just;
All we'll do is just;
All we'll do is just—
Dance!

At the end of the number, HENRY, MOR-TIMER, and MATT have gone, and LUISA and EL GALLO are back in the tree, exactly like the scene before.

EL G: Now hurry. You must pack so that we may run away.

LUISA: Kiss me first.

EL G: All right.

LUISA: Ahh.

EL G: What is it?

LUISA: At last! I have been kissed upon the eyes. No matter what happens, I'll never never ever forget that kiss. I'll go now.

EL G: One word, Luisa, listen:
               I want to tell you this—
               I promise to remember too
               That one particular kiss.
               . . . And now hurry; we have a lifetime for kisses.

LUISA: True. You'll wait here?

EL G: I promise.

LUISA: All right then.

EL G: Wait. Give me a trinket—to pledge that you will come back. That necklace—

LUISA: Was my Mother's.

EL G: Good. It will serve as your pledge.

LUISA: All right. I leave you this necklace because it is my favourite thing. Here, guard it. I won't be long.

SHE starts to go and then turns back.
It's really like that? The world is like you say?
EL G: Of course.
Sings.
"Beyond that road lies a shining world."

And sudenly we see MATT returning. HE is in shadow, and neither LUISA nor EL GALLO take any notice of HIM as HE sings:

MATT: Beyond that road lies despair.
EL G: Beyond that road lies a world that's gleaming.
MATT: People who are scheming.
EL G: Beauty!
MATT: Hunger!
EL G: Glory!
MATT: Sorrow!
EL G: With never a pain or care.
MATT: She's liable to find a couple of surprises there.

LUISA: I'm ready. I won't be long.

Once more, SHE turns back.

You will be here?
EL G: Right here. I promise.

When LUISA has gone, EL GALLO turns to leave. He is interrupted by MATT.

MATT: Wait.
EL G: Well, The Prodigal Son comes home.
MATT: Don't leave her like that.
It isn't fair.
EL G: It's her misfortune,
What do you care?

MATT: She's too young.
I said, don't leave her!

MATT tries to stop him. EL GALLO raises his hand and hits the BOY, knocking him down to his knees, then EL GALLO moves into the shadows at the side.

LUISA returns. SHE calls out for EL GALLO, but HE isn't there. SHE continues to call his name as SHE begins to realize that SHE has been left. Then slowly SHE sinks to her knees, on the opposite side of the stage from MATT. EL GALLO appears from the shadows and addresses the audience.

EL G: There is a curious paradox
That no one can explain.
Who understands the secret
Of the reaping of the grain?

Who understands why Spring is born
Out of Winter's laboring pain?
Or why we all must die a bit
Before we grow again.

I do not know the answer.
I merely know it's true.
I hurt them for that reason
And myself a little bit too.

HE steps back into the shadows.

MATT: It isn't worth tears, believe me.
Luisa, please—don't cry.
LUISA: You look awful.

91

MATT:	I know.
LUISA:	What's that swelling?
MATT:	That's my eye.
LUISA:	Oh. And those scratches. What in the world happened to you?
MATT:	The world happened to me.
LUISA:	Did you drink and gamble?
MATT:	The first day, yes. But the drink was drugged, And the wheel kept hitting sixes. Until I played a six.
LUISA:	Did you serenade señoras?
MATT:	I did for a little while. Until I got hit.
LUISA:	Hit?
MATT:	With a slop pot.
LUISA:	What?
MATT:	A Spanish slop pot. Believe me, it defies description.
LUISA:	*Smiles.* I'm sorry, Matt.
MATT:	No. It's all right. I deserve it. I've been foolish.
LUISA:	I have too. Believe me. More than you.

*And simply—very simply—THEY face each other
and sing:*

MATT:	When the moon was young, When the month was May, When the stage was hung for my holiday, I saw shining lights, but I never knew—

They were you
They were you
They were you.

LUISA: When the dance was done,
When I went my way,
When I tried to find rainbows far away,
All the lovely lights seemed to fade from view—
They were you
They were you
They were you.

BOTH: Without you near me,
I can't see.
When you're near me.
Wonderful things come to be.

Every secret prayer,
Every fancy free,
Every thing I dared for both you and me,
All my wildest dreams multiplied by two,
They were you
They were you
They were you.

Left to right: CAROLE DEMAS as
Luisa, JOE BELLOMO as El Gallo,
STEVE SKILES as Matt, Sullivan
Street production.

LUISA: I missed you, Matt.
MATT: I missed you too.
LUISA: Oh, you've been hurt.
MATT: Yes.
LUISA: But you should have told me.
You should have told me that right away.
Here, sit down. Maybe I can bind it.

THEY sit on the platform, as the MUTE stands above and behind them and sprinkles them with paper "snow."

MATT: You've been hurt, too.
LUISA: Yes.
MATT: It's beginning to snow.
LUISA: I know.
MATT: Here. Take my coat.
LUISA: No. Both.
There's room enough for both.

THEY pull close together and THEY sing.

BOTH: Love.
You are love. (You are love.)
Better far than a metaphor can ever, ever be.
Love—You are love. (You are love.)
My mystery— (My mystery)
of Love—

And the FATHERS, who have been sitting upstage, now rise and come forward.

BELL: Look!
EL G: *Who has watched it all, steps forward.*
Shh.

RICHARD STAUFFER
as the Mute,
original Sullivan
Street production.

HUCK: They've come back.
BELL: It's a miracle. Let's take down the wall.
EL G: No. Leave the wall.
Remember—
You must always leave the wall.

Sings, as the others hum beneath him.

Deep in December, it's nice to remember,
Although you know the snow will follow.
Deep in December, it's nice to remember:
Without a hurt the heart is hollow.
Deep in December, it's nice to remember
The fire of September that made us mellow.
Deep in December, our hearts should remember
And follow.

*And the MUTE gets the "FANTASTICKS" drape
from the prop box. And HE and EL GALLO carefully hang it on the poles in front of the PARENTS
and the LOVERS. And when the stage, in fact, is
as it was in the beginning, the lights dim down. And
the play, of course, is done.*

Celebration

Drawing by HARVEY SCHMIDT of the original setting at Portfolio Workshop.

Celebration

A Musical Fable

Words by
Tom Jones

Music by
Harvey Schmidt

For Cheryl Crawford

Left to right: KEITH CHARLES, TED THURSTON, SUSAN
WATSON, MICHAEL GLENN-SMITH.

Original Cast

CELEBRATION was first presented by Cheryl Crawford and Richard Chandler at the Ambassador Theatre in New York City on January 22nd, 1969, with the following cast.

POTEMKIN .... Keith Charles
ORPHAN .... Michael Glenn-Smith
ANGEL .... Susan Watson
RICH .... Ted Thurston

THE REVELERS

Glenn Bastion	Frank Newell
Cindi Bulak	Pamela Peadon
Stephen deGhelder	Felix Rice
Leah Horen	Sally Riggs
Patricia Lens	Gary Wales
Norman Mathews	Hal Watters

Musical Numbers Staged and
Choreographed by
VERNON LUSBY

Settings, Lighting and Costumes by
ED WITTSTEIN

Musical Direction by
RED DEREFINKO

Orchestration by
JIM TYLER

Production Coordination by
ROBERT ALAN GOLD

Directed by
TOM JONES

GLENN BASTION leading the opening procession in the Original
Broadway production.

Musical Numbers

ACT ONE

CELEBRATION	Potemkin and the Revelers
ORPHAN IN THE STORM	Orphan and the Revelers
SURVIVE	Potemkin and the Revelers
SOMEBODY	Angel and the Devil Girls
BORED	Rich
MY GARDEN	Orphan and the Revelers
WHERE DID IT GO	Rich and the Revelers
LOVE SONG	Angel, Potemkin, Rich, Orphan and the Revelers
TO THE GARDEN	Everyone

ACT TWO

I'M GLAD TO SEE YOU'VE GOT WHAT YOU WANT	Angel, Orphan
IT'S YOU WHO MAKES ME YOUNG	Rich and the Revelers
NOT MY PROBLEM	Potemkin and the Dancing Machines
FIFTY MILLION YEARS AGO	Orphan
THE BEAUTICIAN BALLET	Potemkin and the Revelers
SATURNALIA	Potemkin and the Revelers
UNDER THE TREE	Angel and Girls
WINTER AND SUMMER	Everyone
CELEBRATION (FINALE)	Everyone

KEITH CHARLES as Potemkin, Broadway production.

Act I

A platform, very crudely built and primitive. Above it, a huge sun.

As the time for the ritual draws near, the sun begins to very slowly go into eclipse. Drums are heard. "Telegraph" drums, echoing back and forth from different corners of the auditorium. As the sun gets smaller and smaller, the lights grow progressively more dim. Slowly, slowly, very slowly, the great orb of the sun is blotted into darkness. There is a last, lingering glimmer of a rim, and then the sun is gone. The eclipse is total. The drums, which have been building to fever pitch, abruptly stop.

There is a moment of total darkness and of silence. And then POTEMKIN enters, carrying a torch. Later on he will appear in the story as a cynical bum, but now he wears the simple garment of the Narrator. As the drum starts up again, he mounts the platform and speaks directly to the audience.

POT: In ancient days, in Winter,
When the sun kept sinking lower in the sky,
Men started to wonder if it could die.
"Look", they said:
"The Day is being eaten by the Night!"
"Look," they said:
"The darkness is devouring the Light!"
And they were frightened.

Sings.

Some people say
That today is the day

107

When the wind will rise
And blow the world away.
And it may be so—
I just don't know.
All I know is up until we have to go,
I want to celebrate!
I want to make a celebration!
I want to celebrate!
I want to savour each sensation!
See the sunlight rise;
Feel it touch the sky:
I want to stay alive
Until the day I die!
I want to celebrate
Every day!

*Music continues. And now the REVELERS appear
in procession, making their way up to the platform,
carrying torches and banners and masks. In the
center is an improvised litter, upon which is borne,
half-hidden, the figure of a huge, fat man.*

The Revelers in the Broadway production.

And so the people gathered by the fire.
They drank and sang and made up plays.
They painted their faces, and in the blaze,
They   waited—
Hoping for a sign.

Sings, as REVELERS join in.

Some people say
That tonight is the night
When the bird will fly
And eat away the light;
And it may be so.
I just don't know.
All I know is up until we have to go,
I want to celebrate!
I want to make a celebration!
I want to celebrate!
I want to savour each sensation!
Feel the blazing fire!
Drain the cup of wine.
I want to light the torch and
Teach the sun to shine!
I want to celebrate
Every day!

We're like those ancient people, in a way.
We've gathered by the fire to do a play.
Our night is dark like theirs.
Our world is cold.
Our hopes seem frozen
Underneath the snow—
And yet, if you will just assist us
With your imagination,
We'll try to make this humble stage
A place for
Celebration!

ALL: *Sing.*

Some people say
That today is the day
When the cold will come
And never go away.
When the bird will fly,
The wind will blow,
But something deep inside me says it can't be so.
I want to celebrate!
I want to make a celebration!
I want to celebrate!
I want to savour each sensation.
Something deep inside
　　(Something deep inside)
Says "beneath the snow"
　　(Says "beneath the snow")
"There's a tiny seed."
　　("There's a tiny seed.")
"And it's gonna grow!"
　　("And it's gonna grow!")

I want to celebrate
Every day!
Every day!
Every day!
C-E-L-E-B-R-A-T-I-O-N!
CELEBRATION!

KEITH CHARLES as Potemkin with the Revelers, Broadway production.

POT :   *When the song is over.*

Now—
Imagine if you will a Winter; cold.
So cold that almost no one
Ventures forth upon the snow.
The Time: New Year's Eve.
The Place: A desolate street
On the outskirts of the city.
The characters: A young boy
And an old man,
And of course, a pretty girl.
For this is a fable
An ancient tale.
We tell it again to pass the time
While waiting for the sun.

Music: The BOY steps forward into the light. HE has a nice, goofy face and strange, old-fashioned clothes. As the REVELERS cluster in the darkness, half-hidden, watching, the BOY turns up his collar against the cold and softly begins to sing.

BOY :   Nose—cold.
Toes—froze.
I don't know
Where this road goes.
Way off somewhere
I see light.
If I don't freeze,
I guess I'll be
All right.

*REVELERS begin to whistle softly like the wind
and to throw long white streamers of confetti at the
BOY, as HE sets out on his journey.*

BOY: I could light a fire if I had a match.
I could patch my pants if I had a patch.
I could hurry home but there's just one catch:
I'm an orphan in the storm.

I could bake some beans if I had a pot.
I could heat some tea if the pot was hot.
I could buy a pie, but I just forgot:
I'm an orphan in the storm.

Hey, Mister Sun, hiding in the sky,
Won't you hurry back in sight!
I need some sunshine; I'll tell you why:
Don't know where I'll sleep tonight.

I could catch a bus if I had the fare.
I could catch a cold if I don't take care.
I could catch my death, but I won't despair,
For somewhere it's safe and warm.

Hey, Mr. Somebody in the sky,
Won't you guide me through the storm.

*Dance as the BOY begins to encounter the city.
REVELERS put on the masks of whores, pimps,
addicts, etc., and begin to torment and tease him.
Some of them hold up large placards with city faces
painted on them. Others have New Year's Eve
noisemakers, which they loudly bang and blow.*

REVEL: Psst!
Hey!
Wow!
Happy New Year, honey!
Hey!
Wow!
Ha! Ha!
Ha! Ha!
Sing mockingly.

Hey, Mr. Somebody in the sky,
Better hurry, hurry, hurry down
And save your little orphan boy!
Bring him some sunshine;
We'll show you why:

Cause we're gonna pick his little pocket
And maybe take his little overcoat
Steal his pretty little muffler
And mess around with his virginity!
Catch him
And rob him
And teach him a lesson!
So hurry, hurry, hurry, hurry, hurry,
Little orphan boy!
Better run!
Better run!
Better run!
Ha ha ha ha!

And now the REVELERS make a veritable bliz-
zard of paper "snow" as the YOUNG BOY strug-
gles forward in the dark.

BOY :   I could catch a bus if I had the fare.
I could catch a cold if I don't take care.
I could catch my death, but I won't despair,
For somewhere it's safe and warm.

Hey, Mr. Somebody in the sky.
Won't you guide me through—
Do what you can do—
For this orphan in
The storm!

When the number is over, somebody in the darkness
applauds. It is POTEMKIN, who appears in his
bum outfit, alternately applauding and daubing his
eyes with the dirtiest handkerchief ever seen on the
American stage.

POT: Ah—beautiful! Beautiful! Very touching!

Blows his nose. Loud honk.
Poor little Orphan in the Storm.

BOY: Who are you?

POT: Allow me to introduce myself.—My card.

BOY: *Reads.*

"Please help me. I am blind."

POT: Ooops. Sorry. Wrong card. I'm only blind in the Summer. In the dog days. Here. Try this one.

BOY: *Reads.*

"Po-tem-"

POT: "kin." Alexander J. Potemkin. At your service. Those are nice shoes.

BOY: Shoes?

POT: *On his knees, examining them.*

Oh yes. There's a good five, maybe six, years in those shoes yet. I wonder if I might see one of them for just a minute?

BOY: All right.

POT: It's always such a pleasure to see fine workmanship. Oh, and that scarf, too. Such an interesting design! And let's see, what have we got inside the bag? A Bible. Toilet paper. A package of seeds.

And as POTEMKIN goes through the OR-PHAN's possession, stealing whatever he can find, the lights dim—Music begins—and the YOUNG BOY tells his "story."

BOY: You see, I'm an orphan. I worked inside the garden at the Orphanage. But then a funny thing began to happen. All of the people that I knew when I was

116

younger began to disappear. At first I thought, "Oh well, they've all been adopted!" But then it wasn't just the other orphans. It was the teachers too. And the priests. Until finally there wasn't anybody left at all except me.—And then some men came with big machines, and they began to tear down all the buildings. They had a ball on a great long chain and they swung it—way, way out—above the trees and the garden. And then, when it came back, it smashed into the Face of God.

POT: The Face of God?

BOY nods; POTEMKIN speaks to Audience.

Boy, can I pick 'em!

BOY: Well, I ran over and I took the Eye of God—that was all that was left of the stained glass. Look, I'll show you!

Gets "Eye of God" from his bag and holds it up. Music.

MICHAEL GLENN-SMITH as the Boy and KEITH CHARLES as Potemkin, Broadway production.

I'm going to see the old man.

POT: What!

*And now the Music changes to a nervous drumbeat
as two REVELERS appear with ornate chair and
place it imperiously on the upper platform.*

BOY: He's having a party for New Year's Eve. I'm going
to sneak in. I'm going to tell him what they did to
the chapel. I'm going to make him stop tearing down
buildings. We don't want a factory; we want a
garden!

*POTEMKIN looks at him—looks at the Bible and
the toilet paper. And then, making up his mind, he
pockets the toilet tissue and returns the Bible to the
boy.*

POT: OK. When do we start?

BOY: We?

POT: Well—Have you ever been to a fabulous New
Year's Eve Party?

BOY: No.

POT: Which comes first—the soup or the nuts?

BOY: I don't know.

POT: Who makes the first toast? Host or Guest of
Honor?

BOY: Well, I guess . . .

POT: No, no, no. No guessing! To guess is to hesitate and
to hesitate is to faux-pas.

BOY: To what?

118

POT: Faux-pas! It's a Russian expression. It means "fuck-up."

BOY: Oh.

POT: How do you expect to get up there, on that mountain? How are you going to climb that social scale? Eh? Do you know how to push? How to shove? How to beg? How to bribe? How to crawl? How to creep? How to steal? How to cheat? No! All you know how to do is grow things in a garden. What you need, Little Orphan, is an Adviser. Somebody older. Wiser. A little bit more experienced in the ways of the wicked world.

BOY: *It hits him.*

You!

POT: *Pinching him on the cheek.*

Smart boy!

Sings.

I've been everything that a man could be,
From aristocrat to bum.
I've learned every trick of the beggar's trade.
Why, I've even invented some.
I've soared to the heights,
I've sunk to the depths,
And here's how I stay alive—
When faced with a choice
I say to myself:
"Potemkin, my friend,
Survive.
Just survive."

Sometimes at night
When it is dark,
I spot a pigeon
In the park.
And then I croon:
"Koo-Roo-Koo-Koo"
"Won't you join me in a pigeon stew?"

Sometimes at day
When people pass,
I eat my pride
And kiss their ass.
Down on my knees,
"Kind sir," I squeak,
"Won't you kindly kick the other cheek?"

Time and time again
To myself I say:
"Stand up like a man!
Change the world today!
Fight for what is right!
Die heroically."
Then I start to think
How messy death must be.

So come with me
And I will show
You all the crooked
Tricks I know.
We'll steal and cheat,
And we'll connive.
But it's worth it all
If we survive.

REVELERS begin to put on masks of rich people.

See that rich man there
Looking prosperous.
Just remove his mask,
He's the same as us.
He will steal and cheat
Given half a chance,
But with him they call it
"High finance."

*Music. A dance—as we see various of the REV-
ELERS step forward in masks of the decadent rich.
Some of the masks are frighteningly real; others are
grotesque: apes and moles and rats with emerald
earrings and elaborate tiaras.*

121

POT: Everywhere you go,
It is all the same.
People, high or low,
Play the same old game.
Learn to push and shove,
Carve yourself a niche,
And we'll wind up right on top
With Mr. Rich.

POT
AND
REVEL: So come with us
And we will show
You all the crooked
Tricks we know.
We'll steal and cheat
And we'll connive.
But it's worth it all if we survive.

Maybe we eat mud but we survive!
Maybe we lack pride but we survive!
Maybe we all lie
But we can justify it
With our little motto:
"Do whatever you've got to!"
It is worth it all
If you just stay alive.
Sur-vive!
Just sur—
vive!

Strange music as POTEMKIN and the BOY are
left alone. A large object covered with ragged black
cloth comes sliding into place beside them. Then

another and another until there are a series of such strange, forbidding forms.

BOY: What is it? What's happening?
POT: Shhh.

Speaks to Audience.

"The Dwelling of the Old Man."

Music: Mysterioso.

It's like some sort of castle
Or a cave.
An eerie place—
With glittering bits of tinsel
Hung from rafters
To celebrate the night.
All in all,
It's what you might call:
Gothic.
BOY: Look, there's something crawling on the floor.
POT: *Steps on it.*

Ugh.
BOY: And what are those things—with the cloth in front?
POT: *Looks behind one of the drapes.*

They're mirrors.
BOY: Mirrors! But—why are they covered?
POT: Who knows? Maybe he hates mirrors.
Hey, what are you doing?
BOY: I'm praying.
POT: What! Oh, come on. What are you trying to do, embarrass me? Nobody believes in God anymore.

It's over, kid. The jig is up. There is no Heaven. There is no Hell. There are no little White Lady Angels hovering up in the sky—What's the matter? What are you staring at?

BOY: There's a little white lady angel hovering in the sky.

POT: What?

The BOY points up in the air. POTEMKIN turns to see a beautiful girl with angel wings and halo standing on the upper platform.

Oh my God!

BOY: I think she heard you.

POT: Why me? Eighty million agnostics in the country. Why does she have to pick on me?

BOY: Shh. She's about to speak.

POT: Quick. Kneel again. Just to be safe.

ANGEL: Excuse me. Have either of you guys seen Satan? Or the Devil Girls?

POT: *Unable to believe his ears.*

The "Devil Girls"?

ANGEL: They all have little sparkly tails. And whips.

POT: It's too much. No, this time it's too much.

BOY: Shhh.

ANGEL: Or do you know how I can get down from here?

BOY: Can't you fly.—With your wings?

ANGEL: Oh no. They're breakaways. I'm supposed to be a Fallen Angel. Look, I'll show you.

SHE pulls a string and her Angel outfit does indeed "breakaway," leaving her naked with just a bit of a little spangled devil costume underneath. PO-TEMKIN and the BOY are both quite stunned.

SUSAN WATSON as Angel, Broadway production.

ANGEL:	Spectacular, huh?
POT:	To say the least.
ANGEL:	I'm part of the entertainment, you see. For New Year's Eve. I sing with a group called the Hittites and as we do our big number, the Devil Girls do a kind of whip dance and then—at the climax—I pull my string—and—pow! The only thing is I got stuck up on this goddamn platform.
POT:	Try the railing. We'll stand beneath you, just in case.
ANGEL:	I'm scared.
POT:	Come on. You'll make it.
ANGEL:	Well—Catch my wings, will you? They'll dock me if anything happens to them.

Sits on edge of platform.

	I'm getting dizzy.
POT:	Come on.
ANGEL:	Oh God, why did I ever want to be a star! Look out! Here I come!

She descends into the YOUNG BOY's arms.

Hey, what are you blushing about?

Shyly, the BOY points to her exposed flesh.

Oh—my body! Do you like it?

BOY:	Very much.
ANGEL:	Oh, that's great. You know, for a young actress, having a good body is half the battle. Look, do you see my breasts? They have a tendency to be smallish. I get that from my mother. So I have to do 25 presses every evening at the gym. But I think it's worth it, don't you?—I mean, they turned out nice, don't you think?

126

BOY: They're beautiful.
ANGEL: Oh, gee, thanks! They're still a little small—I mean, by Playboy Standards, for example. But they're on the way. What about my color? Did you notice that?
BOY: Oh, yes!
ANGEL: *Pleased.*

Really? Does it look golden, do you think? My manager wants me to bill myself as the "Golden Goddess." But I don't know. It sounds kind of pushy to me.

Looks at him.

You're got a nice face.
BOY: Really?
ANGEL: Oh, sure. Good teeth. Nice complexion. Sort of a goofy smile. They don't like for juveniles to be too handsome anymore.

By now, ANGEL and the BOY are standing very close, caught in a curious attraction. But suddenly she realizes that more and more REVELERS are pouring onto the stage.

ANGEL: Oh my God!
I've got to go. I'm "on."
BOY: But—will I see you—later?
ANGEL: I don't know. Are you Somebody?

The BOY looks at POTEMKIN.

POT: No. In the way she means, you're Nobody.
ANGEL: I'm sorry, but I can't waste my time on somebody who's Nobody, because of my career.

ANGEL takes her place in the spot-light as the "Hittites" strike up with rock-and-roll music and someone hands her a rather suggestive-looking hand mike.

ANGEL: *Sings.*

At twenty, man you've had it!
If you know what I mean.
And you start aging very fast
The day you reach thirteen!
And so, before these golden days,
These Lolita Days, are through—
I'm gonna get myself some Pucci pants,
And here's what I'm gonna do:

Oslo, Norway, Riksteatret production directed by VERNON LUSBY: SOLFRID HEIER as Angel.

I'm gonna be
Somebody!
Before they lay me in my grave!
I'm gonna be
Somebody!
So everyone'll be my slave!

Why should I sit home alone at night
Shakin' by some broken radiator?
When I could be up there in the light
Shakin' on the stage of some theatre!

I need
Somebody!
Who'll buy me all the things I need
And help me be
Somebody!
Just like the people that I see
Makin' money on tee vee!
Posin' in the magazines!
Dancin' on the movie screen!

*Wild whip dance by ANGEL and the DEVIL
GIRLS.*

ANGEL
AND THE
GIRLS: *Sing.*

Why should I sit home alone at night
Shakin' by some broken radiator?
When I could be up there in the light
Shakin' on the stage of some theatre!

I need
Somebody!

Who'll buy me all the things I need
And help me be
Somebody!
Just like the people that I see
Makin' money on tee vee!
Posin' in the magazine!
Dancin' on the movie screen!

Can't you see
I gotta be
Somebody!

Applause. And then suddenly, it stops.

POT: *To Audience.*

Can you smell it?
Money.
Ah!—
It's funny, isn't it—
The smell of money?
It can cover up
The most obscene of scents.

130

Look—
Observe these people.
No.—Observe me.
My pulse is beating faster.
My heart is thumping.
There's a little trickle of perspiration
Oozing down my arm.
And why?—

MAJOR-
DOMO: Ladies and Gentlemen—
POT: All because of the smell of—

MAJOR-
DOMO: Mr. Edgar—Allen—Rich!
POT: Money!

*REVELERS remove the huge, half-hidden MAN
from behind his umbrella and lower him laboriously
off the edge of the upper platform. Then, THEY
lower his chair. And finally HE sits and we see him
at last: EDGAR ALLEN RICH. HE's bigger
than life. His eyes are extremely mournful—limpid
—but capable of changing instantly to steely cold-
ness or to an unbelievably violent wildness. One senses
about him that love-hate power of the madman—or
the dictator. HE has a moustache, which makes him
look like—who?—no—not Hitler—someone else—
someone out of the pages of American magazines and
newspapers—some famous entrepreneur. No matter.
Right now, HE sits, hunched forward in his glittering chair, eyeing the assemblage with a jaundiced
eye. A long, thin strand of hair hangs forward from
his otherwise balding head. Everyone waits uneasily
for him to speak.*

*RICH signals and one of the REVELERS ties a
little napkin around his neck. Then—at another signal—the REVELER gets a huge boiled lobster and
puts it in the platter in front of RICH—Again, the
expectant silence—RICH picks up the metal crush-
ers and with a slow, disdainful "crunch"—HE
cracks into the crustacean.*

RICH: Urp.
             Faw.
             Plog!

             Sings.

             If you could see the inside of my stomach—
             I think it might just take your breath away.

             Crunch.

TED THURSTON (left) as Rich and GARY WALES as the Major-
Domo, Broadway production.

But no matter how I diet—
It simply won't stay quiet—
It's like some sort of riot—
Or like a fiery blast
On judgment day!

Crunch.

My blood pressure?
You ask me:
What about my blood pressure?

Crunch.

My cardiogram reads like some comic opera plot.

Crunch.

I cannot sleep.
I cannot eat.
And none of those stupid goddam doctors has the
Slightest idea what I've got!
Orugh.—
Aplruugh!
Agh! Agh!

*This last as HE spits up part of the lobster onto the
floor.*

Where did you catch that thing? In the Holland
Tunnel? Get it out of here!

*And HE hurls the remains of the lobster off to the
side as the music picks up a delicate syncopated
rhythm.*

When I've got a terrible hunger—
Feeling the need to be eating—
I just press the bell in my dining room;
All at once it's teeming with gastronomes
Who prepare the rarest of recipes:
Peacock's tails and truffles from Tuscany
Stuffed into a boar's head from Borneo
Glazed on top with blazing tomato paste.
When they cut the tongue out—
I'm bored!
Bored!
Bored!
Bored!

When I'm in a state of depression—
Craving some fresh titillation—
I just dial the world's finest inter-com:
Instantly they send exhibitionists
Who perform the latest atrocities
Meant to whet the deadest of appetites.
As they show each sexy spectacular,
And erect each pulsating pyramid,
Rising to a climax—
I'm bored!
Bored!
Bored!
Bored!

I'm the richest man in the western world:
There is nothing I can't afford!

I'm the president of the stock exchange:
I'm the chairman of every board!

I've got everything that they say it takes:
But no matter how much I hoard—

I'm bored, bored, bored, bored!
I'm bored, bored, bored, bored!
Boo-pee boo-pee Boop!
I'm
B—bump—
O—bump—
R—bump—
E—D—
Bored!
God, how I'm bored!
Calls out, after the song is over:
Everything around me is dark and cold. I'm bored!

VOICE: *From the shadows, sings out.*

        The sun!

RICH: Everything around me is Winter-time and ice.
        I'm bored!

VOICE: *Sings.*

        The sun!

RICH: All of the trees are leafless—Bones.
        I'm bored!

MICHAEL GLENN-SMITH
as the Boy, Broadway
production.

VOICE: *Sings.*

The sun!
The sun!
The sun!

And the BOY steps out into the light, holding up the Eye of God, which sparkles like the sunlight. RICH looks at him, fascinated.

RICH: What are you? A performer?
BOY: I'm an orphan.

Music. And the REVELERS pull back in awe.

RICH: What's that thing?
BOY: It's the Eye of God.

Music. REVELERS and DEVIL GIRLS cower in the shadows.

RICH: *Looking at BOY suspiciously.*

Oh.

Oslo, Norway, Riksteatret production, left to right: BJORN SKAGESTAD as the Boy, PER SKIFT as Potemkin, JONAS BRUN-VOLL as Rich.

RICH: What do you mean?
POT: Look at his face. No, no, no. Not like that!
Look at it through that thing.

Holds up "Eye of God."

This is no ordinary face, Mr. Rich.

RICH: *To Audience.*

It's true.
POT: I'll question him. Observe.—Hey, kid, what do you
do when you go to bed at night?
BOY: I say my prayers.
POT: And then what?
BOY: I go to sleep.
POT: What about you, Mr. Rich? What do you do when
you go to bed at night? Do *you* go to sleep, Mr.
Rich?

Points to the BOY.

Maybe he knows something we don't know. Or
have forgotten. Maybe he can make you feel again!
RICH: I don't believe it.
POT: Try.

To the BOY, sotto vocce.

Sing.
BOY: The sun!
The sun!
The sun!
RICH: How much will it cost me?
POT: How much you want to feel?
RICH: The whole works.

BOY: It isn't all dark. The world isn't all dark.
RICH: No?
BOY: It's balanced.
RICH: You mean, there's a beautiful rainbow at the end of the sky of grey?
BOY: Something like that.
RICH: When you walk through the storm, hold your head up high?
BOY: That's right, yes.
RICH: Though April showers may come your way—
BOY: They *do* bring flowers.
RICH: Um-hm. Come over here.—No.—Closer.

HE's face to face with the BOY now. Nose to nose.

You want to know a secret?
BOY: Sir?
RICH: I haven't had an erection in 25 years.—
What do you think about that?
BOY: I don't know, sir.
RICH: *Imitates his voice—mockingly.*

"I don't know, sir." "I don't know, sir." I haven't laughed in 25 years. I haven't cried in 25 years. I haven't felt anything—*not anything at all*—in almost a quarter of a century. So, do you know what I say? I say you can just take that Eye of God and you can shove it up your ass!

To his men.

Now get him out of here.
POT: Wait! When you were talking to the kid here, Mr. Rich, were you bored?

138

BOY: You bought some land to turn into a factory. I want to have it back.

RICH: Okay. Make me feel.

A pause. The BOY looks over at POTEMKIN, uncertain what to do next.

POT: It's all right. Don't get nervous. Come over here and stand on the box.—That's it. The rest of you stay back.

BOY: *Sees ANGEL.*

Hi!

POT: Concentrate! Come on tell him about your garden, like you did with me. He'll be interested.

RICH: Yeah, I lived in a garden once, when I was a kid. Or a farm. Something like that. I don't remember what the hell it was.

POT: You see!

To one of the REVELERS, who just happens to be holding an auto-harp.

Give him a "G."

BOY: Well—

And the BOY holds the Eye of God as the lights dim and the REVELERS form a glittering, half-hidden tableau behind him. On either side, young, half-clothed teeny-boppers are licking long, suggestive-looking suckers and listening wide-eyed.

Sings.

My garden.
My garden.
Each seed conceals a mystery.

139

My garden.
My garden.
Each season has its history.

Reaching for the sun!
Dying when the time
Has come.

My garden.
My garden.
How patiently it teaches me:

Summertime—
Wintertime—
Are one—!

RICH: *As the Music continues underneath.*

That's beautiful. Do it again.

To the REVELERS.

You—do it with him.

ANGEL: But—Mr. Rich—we don't know the words.

POT: *Moving in.*

Perfectly all right. I'll teach them.

RICH: Good.

*And as the BOY sings, ANGEL, REVELERS and
POTEMKIN join in with a sort of honeyed har-
mony, one phrase behind him.*

BOY
AND
REVEL: My garden.
    (My garden!)

140

My garden.
   (My garden!)
Each seed conceals a mystery!

RICH: Sensational.

BOY
AND
REVEL: My garden.
   (My garden!)
My garden.
   (My garden!)
Each season has its history.

RICH: *Directing the chorus, like Fred Waring.*

Baritones!

BARIT: "Reaching for the sun!"
RICH: Sopranos!
SOPRAN: "Dying when the time has come!"
RICH: Now—everybody!
CHORUS: My garden!
   (My garden!)
My garden!
   (My garden!)
How patiently it teaches me:

Summertime—
Wintertime—
Are one—!

RICH: *Sings, off-key.*

"Summertime—wintertime—"
Son of a bitch. That's beautiful! Do some more!
BOY: But that's all there is.

141

RICH: I said: Do some more!
BOY: Well—

Sings.

Summer—
Autumn—
Winter—
Spring—

I know
Just what
The year
Will bring.
I plow;
I plant;
I reap;
And then;
It's summer—
Autumn—
Winter—
Spring—
All over again!

*And as HE sings this bouncy little verse again—the
decadent young "swingers" pick it up.*

RICH: Now—do the middle part. That really gets me.
ALL: Reaching for the sun!
        Dying when the time has come!

*And somehow the pure little song has picked up a
rock-and-roll beat along the way.*

Revelers in the Maracaibo,
Venezuela, Teatro Real production.

My garden!
My garden!
How patiently it teaches me:
Summertime—(summertime)
Wintertime—(wintertime)
Are one!
Yeah, yeah, yeah, yeah!

At the end of the number, a brief silence. Then—a strange sound.

POT: *Stepping forward, anxiously.*

Mr. Rich . . .

RICH: Shhh!

POT: Mr. Rich, are you all right?

RICH: Quiet! I think—I'm—about—to—feel—something!

There is a gasp from the CROWD.

RICH: Sing.

REVEL: *Sing—rock-and-roll version.*

"My garden! My garden!"

RICH: No. Not so loud. Soft!

REVEL: *Sing—soft version.*

"My garden! My garden!"

RICH: Hum.

THEY hum.

Oh—oh!

Then—a long, dry, rasping contraction of a sob, followed by a delicate "plink" of Music.

RICH: Oh my God! Look!

HE holds up something glistening on his finger-tip.

POT: A tear-drop!

Another gasp from the CROWD.

RICH: It's evaporating. Quick! Do something!
POT: Here's a plastic bag!
RICH: No, no—you dumbbell. You can't package a tear-drop. Get me an ice box. Maybe we can freeze it!

And POTEMKIN and the REVELERS start scurrying around.

POT: Ice box! Ice box!

RICH: *A cry of agony.*

Agh!
POT: Mr. Rich, what is it?
RICH: Too late! It's gone! My one tear and you let it get away. Oh, Time—you old bastard!

Shakes his fist.

You did it again, didn't you?

Suddenly, to the BOY.

Do me another one!
Who are you anyway? What magic power have you got that you can suddenly make me feel?

Suddenly struck.

Wait! Now I know!
Now I know who you look like—who it is you remind me of.
BOY: Who?

RICH: Me!

BOY: *Horrified.*

You?

RICH: Yes, me! Thirty years ago. Oh God, look at that youth—that innocence—that beautiful stupidity. Wait! I think—I'm about to—Stand back!

Music: Another delicate "Plink."

I did it again! Look at that! Two in a row! I'm feeling again! Ha. Ha.

HE shows the new tear to the CROWD.

145

I know what it is now. I know what's happening.
I'm seeing my whole life pass in front of my eyes.
Oh God—it's pitiful! Aah! Light! Give me that
spotlight!

*HE pushes the BOY aside and steps into the pool
of light. One or Two REVELERS rush off and
return with instruments—out-of-tune violin, etc.*

*Then, as RICH tells his story, THEY play a senti-
mental accompaniment in the background.*

RICH: Thirty years ago I was poor. Like him. I didn't
have a nickel, but still I was a happy man. I woke up
each morning like a little bird. When the sun come
up, I said, "Hello, Sun!" I was a dancer in the
morning sunlight. And a laugher in the afternoon!
Ah!—What happened?—
I'll tell you what happened. I came out into the
world, that's what happened! I became a millionaire.
That's what happened! Here. Look at this!

*MAJOR-DOMO appears and hands him some-
thing.*

BOY: What is it?
RICH: Falsies. Ladies' bosoms. Go on, touch it. Feel that
spring. That texture. Kiss it! Smell it! That's how
I made my first million. On falsies. Then I ex-
panded. I got into artificial limbs. Glass eyes. And
then false teeth. And finally, artificial fruits and
flowers.

BOY: You mean, you *made* a flower?
RICH: Did I make a flower? Take a look at that!

Gets flower from MAJOR-DOMO.

Look at that stamen. That cute little pistil.
I'd like to know who makes a better.

BOY: God does.

RICH: God?—
Don't make me laugh.
You had a garden. Tell me—
How long did your flowers last?
One spring?

BOY: And summer, too.

RICH: All right.
One spring and summer.
Look at this, kid:
I bang it on the floor!
I kick it!
I jump up and down on top of it!
What happens? Nothing!
You can buy this flower on the day you get married,—
And get this:
They can use the same one when they shovel you under.
How's that for a bargain?

BOY: It doesn't smell.

RICH: You want a smell? Here, I make artificial flower smells, too.

147

Sprays plastic flower.

Oh yes. Yes. Yes. Yes. Yes. I made everything.
And everything I made made money. That's when I
began to have the spells.

BOY : Spells?

RICH : The first thing I noticed was the clocks:
They started going faster.
I'd look down at my desk for a couple of minutes
And then—when I'd look up—
It would be six hours later!
Whole days started—whizzing—by;
I'd turn the page in the paper
And it would be two weeks later!
Or I'd put out my summer wardrobe,
And the snow would start to fall.
And then—
Then—
It got to the point
Where years were slipping by.
I went into the bathroom one morning
And—My God!—
There was somebody there I didn't know!
Some stranger—with jowls—
And blotches on his skin.
And little red veins in the eyes.
And a varicose nose.
Ugh!
That's when I had the mirrors covered up—
And I've never looked in one since.

Music.

Oh God—you should have seen me once! What I

was! I was Father Time's sweet golden darling little
boy.

Sings.

Once upon a time
Not so long ago
I was quite a boy:
A Romeo.

Once upon a beach
In my underwear
All the ladies used to
Stop and stare!

Hair upon my head!
Hair upon my chest!
Everyone I met
Was so impressed.

Hair upon my chin!
Hair upon my brow!
Why am I so damned
Un-hairy now?

*And now FOUR REVELERS, wearing masks of
youth step out with top hats and canes, and begin to
dance behind RICH.*

Where did it go—oh—oh?
Those little locks of mine?
Those teeth that used to shine?

Where is it at—at—at?
Those Shirley Temple dimples?
And that baby fat?

Oh, where has it gone—on—on?
That style so debonair?
That slender derriere?

Oh, where can it be?
Oh, where can it be?
I can't believe
This beast I see
Is really me.
I'm twenty-three.

Sob.

150

Once upon a moon
In the month of May
I chased every dame
That came my way.

Once upon a couch
Or in a canoe
Oh, the naughty things
I used to do!

Speaks over the music.

Ah—what a line I had! What daring! What results!

Chuckles wickedly.

My little nursery maid! Ha. ha.
The Scout Master's wife.
That was a merit badge, all right!
The House Mother at my fraternity!
The Girl's Hockey Team from Bennington, Ver-
mont!
Those Siamese Twins from far-away Peru!!

RICH
AND
REVEL: Oh, where did it go—oh—oh—oh—oh?
That fabulous parade
Of maidens that I made?

Where did it pass—ass—ass?
Those many scenes of
Tender splendor in the grass?

Oh, where did it fly—ai—ai—ai—ai?
Those endless one-night stands?
Those ever-ready glands?

Oh, where can it be?
Oh, where can it be?
Who could believe
I'd live to see
Senility
Reach out for me!

*Again, HE dances pathetically, as the REVELERS
back him up.*

RICH
AND
REVEL: Life's a masquerade—
Crazy game we play.
Neath the painted face,
We waste away.
On and on it goes—
Till the curtains close.

Ten minutes ago I was only a kid;
I was kiddin' around with the gals.
Ten minutes ago I was John Barrymore;
But now look at me: covered with jowls!

I don't know what happened: I looked in the glass,
But instead of me, what did it show?
Some horrible, faded-out, balding old fart—
So now there's one thing I must know:

Where did it go?
Where in the hell—
Did the whole thing
Go?

Ah Dio!

Sobs.

RICH: *After the song.*

I can't stand it any longer!
Somebody get me a pistol!

POTEMKIN gets pistol from coat pocket and hands it to him. RICH raises it to his head.

Goodbye, world.

Pulls trigger. A flag springs out with the word "BANG!"

Agh! Get me a knife.

Throws down pistol in disguest. POTEMKIN hands him rubber knife.

Goodbye, world!

Stabs himself. Nothing.

TED THURSTON as Rich,
Portfolio Workshop
production.

Argh! Get me a rope.

POTEMKIN holds noose for him, as HE slips it around his neck and prepares to jump off box.

Goodbye, world!

HE jumps. Noose breaks. Finally, in a rage, RICH runs to the upper platform and starts to jump.

BOY: Don't do it. Live!

RICH: *On the very brim.*

What? What was that?

BOY: *Live!*
RICH: *"Live"?* What is there to live for?
BOY: The new year! Summer!
RICH: I don't see it.
BOY: It's all around you. Look.

The first of a series of placards on poles is carried in by one of the REVELERS. In bold, crude graphics, there is a picture of a bright green leaf.

See!
Leaves and fields
Already bursting out with green!
RICH: You see that?
BOY: Yes.
RICH: Where? Where is it?
All I see is ice.

HE looks at the placard. Immediately, it is reversed —so that we see, instead of Summer, the grim white image of Winter.

BOY: Keep trying! Look!

Another placard with an image of Summer. But again, it is reversed to Winter just as RICH looks at it.

RICH: No. It's hopeless.
BOY: Sunburst!
RICH: Snowstorm!
BOY: Flowers!
RICH: Thorns!
BOY: Youth!
RICH: Age!
BOY: The sun!
       The sun!
       The sun!
RICH: *Stop it!*

HE grabs BOY by the neck.

Why can you see it and I can't? Why do you have everything and I have nothing?—Argh! Argh!

Suddenly collapses—rigid. HE is having a seizure.

POT: *Immediately taking charge.*

Quick. Get him upstairs. I'll be right there.

To BOY.

Now, listen—you want to get that garden back?
BOY: Oh, yes! I'll do anything.
POT: Then listen to me. You've got to make him see it. You've got to make him feel alive again.—To discover.—To feel that he's like you.
BOY: But *how?*
POT: I don't know how. That's the problem. You—

	Angel—come over here. You want to be Somebody, right?
ANGEL:	Right.
POT:	*Counting it off on his fingers.*

You want to be Somebody. You want your garden.
And he wants to feel alive.—
There must be some way I can pull all of that to-
gether.
Ah ha!

BOY:	What?
POT:	What is it the man said—"The play's the thing . . ."
BOY:	What do you mean?
POT:	You remind him of himself when he was young. Right?
BOY:	Right.
POT:	All right then. Here's what you do. You play a scene—You and you. You pretend to fall in love. You discover each other. You touch. You kiss. You—Wait!

Suddenly, to ANGEL.

You know any love songs?

ANGEL:	Sure. I mean, I guess so.
POT:	All right then. When I tell you—sing one! He's a sucker for music.

Starts up the steps.

ANGEL:	One question.—What's in it for you?
POT:	Did you ever work tent shows? Circuses? Carnivals? No? Well, it's nice. Everybody gets excited. Color. Razz-ma-tazz. Magic! (*Produces a flower out of the air.*) Then, after a while, something begins to

happen. People catch on to your tricks. Even the kids. And your hands get shaky. And the autumn comes along, and you start to think: Better get out. Now! Pull off one big trick and get yourself a cushy spot for life.—Okay. You two just hold the fort down here. Ad-lib a few things till I get him ready.

POTEMKIN hands flower to the BOY then goes off to the upper platform, leaving BOY and ANGEL alone.

ANGEL: I don't know. I mean, I really don't. Six years of ballet. Not to mention tap. And modern. Acting lessons. A vocal coach. Working out in the gym.

Sighs wearily.

Maybe I ought to get out of show business.

BOY: *Looking at the placard.*

Why can I see it and he can't?

ANGEL: A crummy apartment downtown. I told the landlord, I said to him: "Listen, if you don't get the heat fixed, I'm gonna call the rent commission." But of course, I didn't do it.

Odense, Denmark, Odense Teatre production directed by ROGER SULLIVAN: OLE MOLLEGAARD as the Boy, LANE LIND as Angel.

BOY: All he sees is Winter.
ANGEL: Nothing matters anyway.
BOY: Summer is here.
ANGEL: The Bomb.—Show Business.
BOY: It's here inside us.
ANGEL: Nothing.

THEY look at each other blankly.

ANGEL: I think we're in different plays.

Smiles.

Do you know any love songs?
BOY: No.
ANGEL: That's okay. I'll teach you one of mine.
I'll do it through once, and then you can pick it up from that.

Looks at him.

It's a shame, though, in a way.
BOY: What is?
ANGEL: You and me. I mean, like in the good old days: Boy. Girl. Whammo. We'd be halfway to the sack by this time. But it's different now. They want things more realistic. And, realistically speaking, it would never work. We're too different. Take our backgrounds, for example. You grew up green. But my life wasn't like that. I grew up grey.
BOY: Grey?
ANGEL: I lived in a grey house, and I had a grey mother and a grey father, and I went to a grey high school and studied Grey's Shorthand so I could be a grey little secretary all my dull, grey life. But I'm not going to

158

do it! I mean, maybe I'm not the "golden goddess," like my agent says. But I am going to be the golden *something*!

SHE stands for a moment, caught up in her dream. Then the BOY comes over to her and offers her the flower. Touched, ANGEL smiles at him.

POT: Okay. Do the love scene. Come on. Hurry up!
ANGEL: Okay, Okay. Don't get nervous.

To BOY.

Are you ready?

HE nods.

I'll take it through once on my own, and then later on, you can pick it up.
POT: Do a dance too!
ANGEL: In a minute!

To MUSICIANS.

Okay—From the top.

And dutifully, ANGEL and the BOY rise and take their places for a standard love song.

ANGEL: *Sings.*

This is a love song.
Made up of moments—
Made up of moments that
We've never known together.

This is a love song
Composed of longings—
And secret daydreams where
We swear to love forever.

Oslo, Norway, Riksteatern production: BJORN SKAGESTAD as the Boy and SOLFRID HEIER as Angel.

A song of laughter
And sweet desire—
A secret melody in me
That you inspire.

Since I first saw you,
The song's been growing—
And now that you are close
It's almost overflowing!

Come join the chorus!
Come sing beside me!
Come share my love song!

*And THEY dance, joined by several of the REV-
ELERS dressed in green.*

POT: *Sings from above.*

Keep it up; don't stop.
Make believe you're falling in love.
Passion!
Make believe you're burning with passion.

Keep it going!
Keep it soaring!
La-de-da-da-da-de-da-da!
Con amore!

Oh how lovely!
Such emotion!
How romantic!
This is magic!

*And suddenly there is a bold "shift" in the tone of
the music: a new feeling of intensity. And suddenly
the lights on stage begin to change—to become
more soft and dream-like. And suddenly the REV-*

ELERS begin to hold up placards and banners with the images of Summer upon them. Green. Green. Everything is turning into green.

POT: Can't you see:
     The stage is changing!
RICH: Can it be
     It's me who's changing?
POT: Can't you feel
     The fire igniting?
RICH: I believe I feel a spark.

And as the BOY and GIRL kiss and the REV-ELERS begin to hum in the background, RICH grows more and more "involved."

RICH: *Sings.*

Slowly rising.
Slowly rising.
Something deep inside is
Slowly rising:
Tickling me.
Tickling me.
A tiny flame
Is tickling me.
Slowly growing.
Slowly growing.
There's a sign of life
That's slowly showing:
Tickling me.
Tickling me.
Inside my thighs,
It's tickling me.

*And now it becomes contrapuntal, with the BOY
singing "Love Song" and RICH singing "Slowly
Rising" as POTEMKIN urges them on, and
ANGEL and the REVELERS dance.*

RICH: Slowly rising
Slowly rising
Sap inside the
vine is
Slowly rising.
Tickling me—
Tickling me—
Delicious liquid
Tickling me!

BOY: A song of laughter—
And sweet desire—
A secret melody in me
That you inspire!

POT: Keep it up,
Keep it up, don't stop!

RICH: Slowly rising.
Slowly rising.
Deep inside, the
fire is
Slowly rising.
Tickling me—
Tickling me—
The fire of life is
Tickling me!

BOY: Since I first saw
you—
The song's been
growing—
And now that you
are close
It's almost
Overflowing!

POT: Con amore!

RICH: Now I feel it—
Building to a fire!

POT: Oh, how lovely!

RICH: Now I feel it—
Burning with
desire

BOY: Come join the
chorus—
Come sing beside
me—
Come share my
Love song!

POT: Such emotion!

RICH: Tickling me.
          Tickling me.
          That old inferno
          Tickling me.
POT: Keep it up! Keep it up!
          Don't stop!
          Now you're on your own!

RICH
AND
BOY: *Sing together as ANGEL dances between them.*

          A song of laughter—
          And sweet desire.
          A secret melody in me
          That you inspire!

          Since I first saw you—
          The song's been growing.
          And now that you are close
          It's almost overflowing.
          Come join the chorus!
          Come sing beside me!
          Come share—
BOY: My love song!

ANGEL: *Moving toward him.*

          Love song!
RICH: Love song!
ALL: Lo-ve-ve-ve- song!

          *ANGEL pauses for a moment, torn between the
          two men; and then—just on the last bit of music,
          SHE turns to RICH and rushes to him. HE is
          overjoyed.*

RICH: I see it! I see it! Look!

Music.

Leaves and trees already bursting out with green!
And look!

Music.

          A beautiful young girl reaching out her arms to *me*!
POT: Reach out your arms.

SHE does and they are instantly covered with jewels.

ANGEL: *Delighted.*

          Ooh!
RICH: And you. Have you ever handled a big pageant?

POT: *Groveling.*

          Of course. I used to be a theatrical producer.
RICH: All right, then. I'm putting you in charge of the
entertainment for New Year's Eve.

*Takes "Chain of Office" from MAJOR-DOMO
And puts it around POTEMKIN's neck.*

          How much time—until midnight?
POT: A little over an hour.
RICH: All right then. Come on, let's go!
ANGEL: But Mr. Rich.—Where to?
RICH: To the garden, that's where to. We're gonna ring
the New Year in out there, surrounded by flowers,
and dancing! And then—at midnight—You and

          me—
ANGEL: Yes?
  RICH: I've got a surprise.
          Come on and see!

          And RICH and the OTHERS burst out with the
          rock-and-roll version of "My Garden" as THEY
          form a procession and exit from the stage. First,
          POTEMKIN, in his new role as Major-Domo.
          Then RICH and ANGEL, wearing her jewels.
          And finally, the REVELERS, carrying the images
          of green.

   ALL: *Sing.*

          My garden!
          My garden!
          How patiently it teaches me.
          Summertime—!
          Wintertime—!
          Are one.
          Are one, yeah, yeah, yeah, yeah!
          Are one
          Are one, yeah, yeah, yeah!
          Are one—are one—are one—

Drawing by HARVEY SCHMIDT, Portfolio Workshop production.

And finally, THEY are gone—their voices faded into the distance. Only the young BOY is left on the stage, alone. HE finds the flower which ANGEL has left behind, and, softly, HE begins to sing.

BOY: A song of laughter—
And sweet desire—
A secret melody in me
That you inspire.

Then, from the side is heard a "Psst." It is PO-TEMKIN, who emerges from the shadows, holding a piece of paper.

POT: She sent you a note. She wants to meet you early—ahead of the others—at the garden.
BOY: What about?
POT: Who knows?
BOY: Do you think?
POT: Could be!
BOY: Or even—?
POT: Why not?
BOY: Really?
POT: Of course!
BOY: Oh thank you! Thank you! I knew you were my friend!

And HE runs off, following the others, singing as HE goes;

Love Song!
Love Song!
Love Song!

A pause. Then POTEMKIN turns to the Audience.

POT: You know, when I was a magician, I never had a big number. Oh, I could do prophecies—things like that. An occasional levitation. But I dreamed of sawing a lady in half—Ah, what a finish!—Well, I worked on that routine for almost seven years. Twenty-three different partners. Oh, I could do the sawing part all right. That was easy. It was the other part—the getting her back together—that was the real trick. Well, anyway, I learned one little bit of wisdom, and this seems to be an appropriate time to pass it on to you.—You can saw all you want to. But you never know how the trick's turned out till you see the second half.

Music. As HE closes the curtain to the inner below. And ACT ONE is over.

Act II

Entr'acte

As the audience begins to come back from the Intermission, the REVELERS start drifting onto the stage. They (the REVELERS, not the audience) carry little toy musical instruments—recorders and triangles and miniature trumpets and accordions and various "rhythm-band" clickers and drums.

When all of the REVELERS have assembled and are busily (and loudly) engaged in "tuning up," POTEMKIN suddenly sweeps onto the stage, carrying a score and a baton. Majestically, HE raps for their attention, and then, with exquisite finesse, HE conducts the REVELERS in a nursery school version of "My Garden," ending with a great flourish of bowing, by both the Maestro and his "Orchestra."

Then the REVELERS withdraw and the real orchestra picks up the song gently in the background.

KEITH CHARLES as Potemkin, SUSAN WATSON as Angel, Broadway production.

Music: *Very gentle and haunting.*

POT: *Speaks—over music.*

Things change. It may not seem like it, but things *do* change. Take for example the set. Act One took place in the city. Act Two takes place in the country.—In the Young Boy's Garden. Only now it's almost midnight—so the garden is dark and cold.

Lights dim up, cold and grey, on a few bare poles.

The Boy is changing. He's losing some of his innocence.

The BOY steps out.

The Girl has changed from rags to riches.

ANGEL steps out—now even more covered with jewels—and wearing a white fox stole.

The Music is changing—from "cynical" to "soft." If you listen carefully, you can even hear the keys change. Shh.—You see.

Music: Change of Key as the BOY and ANGEL move closer together.

BOY: I got your note.—That you wanted to see me.
ANGEL: I just wanted you to know that it's going to be all right. About your garden. I'll speak to Eddie.
BOY: Eddie?
ANGEL: Mr. Rich.
BOY: Oh. Thank you.
ANGEL: Don't mention it.

Music.

BOY: I guess you're gonna be Somebody now.

ANGEL: And I guess you'll stay here—in your garden.

BOY: And I guess we'll never see each other again.

ANGEL: No. I guess not.

BOY: Well—

ANGEL: Well—

BOY: *Sings.*

I'm glad to see
You've got what you want.
All of your dreams came true.

ANGEL: I'm glad to see
You looking so well,
Happiness goes with you.

BOTH: Once in a while
I start to recall—
When we were both so blue.
I traded dreams with you.
Now look how grand you are!
My, but you've travelled far!

I'm glad to see
You've got what you want.
Your star is rising high.
Here is my hand.
Best wishes and
Goodbye—

ANGEL: *Over the music.*

So, this is your garden, huh?

BOY: Yes.

SHE surveys the scene, but is definitely not impressed. Then, suddenly SHE sneezes.

BOY: God bless you.

ANGEL: Thanks. It's the diamonds. They get a little chilly in the winter.

BOTH: I'm glad to see
(I'm glad to see)
You got what you want.
(You got what you want.)
Your star is rising high.
(Your star is rising high.)
Here is my hand.
(Here is my hand.)
Best wishes and
(Best wishes and)
Goodbye—
(Goodbye)
Goodbye—
(Goodbye)
Goodbye!

When the number is over, THEY stand there— still holding each other by the hand.

POT: Psst.—He's coming!—

But THEY do not move.

And he's got some people with him.—Wow!

But the BOY and GIRL are "frozen," absorbed in each other.

He's wearing a fedora!
And spats!
And look, he's dancing the carioca!
Ladies and Gentlemen—
Let's hear it for that game little millionaire:
Mr. Edgar—!
Allen—!

BOY: I've got to tell you something.
ANGEL: No. Don't! Please!
POT: Rich!

Fanfare.

And RICH comes sweeping on.

RICH: Guess who I am. Go on: Guess.
ANGEL: Fred Astaire?
RICH: No, no. Not him. He's a hoofer. I'm a hero.
And look at these people. Guess who they are:
ANGEL: Hairdressers?
RICH: *No.* They're Decorators. Not *In*terior Decorators.
They're *Ex*terior Decorators.—Why do you think
I moved us all out here to the garden? Because it's
Eden, that's why! Oh, not the way it is now, not a
crappy field full of dead trees. But the way it could
be. Look!

Music: A chord.

176

Artificial flowers. Thousands of them from my factories. And look!

Music: A chord.

A plastic waterfall! And this—This is my masterpiece! Look!

Music: An elaborate fanfare as REVELERS reveal wierd "objet d'art."

ANGEL: What is it?

RICH: What do you mean "what is it?" It's a tree. An artificial tree. We're going to have a costume ball out here for New Year's Eve. Dancing girls! And Father Time! A pageant depicting "New Year's Eve in Many Lands." I've got Potty here in charge of the whole thing.—And then—at midnight—just as the clock strikes twelve—he calls out "Woman!"—And you step out—dressed as Eve—

ANGEL: Eve? You mean like in the Bible?

RICH: Yes. Here's your fig leaf. Then he calls out "Man!" And *I* step out in *my* fig leaf! And then, as the clock strikes twelve, we're going to go behind that tree and we're gonna *eat the forbidden fruit!*

ANGEL: Oh, no!

RICH: Oh, yes! How about that, eh. At my age! But you see, that's the miracle. I'm young again. It's you, you see—

Sings.

It's you who makes me young
When I start feelin' old.
It's you who makes me sunny
When the autumn turns to gold.

177

And when the seasons change,
And the winter's on its way,
Then it's you who makes me dance,
Makes me celebrate each da-aa-ay!
It's you—
It's you—
Who makes me young!

It's you who makes me smile:
Without you I would frown.
It's you who takes my worried face
And turns it upside down.
It's you who makes me bright
On the days when I feel blue.
And if you should go away
Then I don't know what I'd do—oo!
It's you—
It's you—
Who makes me young!

Calls out over music.

Come on, you sissy bastards. Decorate!

*Music grows wilder. An explosion of sound as
"DECORATORS" dance gaily and string the stage
with tatty plastic flowers. RICH grabs ANGEL
and shouts over the music.*

Are you ready?
Arriba—Riba!

*And HE whirls ANGEL into a dance, spinning
about elaborately to impress her with his youth. As
the dance gets wilder, RICH's breathing becomes
more labored.*

Gasping for breath.

Agh, Agh!

"Scoobi-Doobi!"

And HE grabs ANGEL again, dancing harder and harder as his breathing becomes more desperate.

Agh. Agh.
Hootchy-Kootchy!

Agh—Agh!
Hot Tamale!
Agh—Agh!
Barbarriba!
Agh—Agh!
Guacomole!

Grabs ANGEL, and again the dance grows more and more frantic.

RICH's breathing now is almost choked.

Agh—Agh!
"Malaguena!"

Agh!—Agh!
"Boogie—Woogie!"

Agh!—Agh!
"Vincent Lopez!"

Agh! Agh!
Agh! Agh!
Agh! Agh!
Arrgh!
Phew!

Odense, Denmark, Odense
Teatre production:
GERT BASTIAH as Rich,
LANE LIND as Angel.

Then, just before HE collapses, the DECORAT-ORS pick RICH up and shove him back into the fray, dragging him along as THEY sing to ANGEL.

DECOR: It's you who make him smile.
Without you he would frown.
It's you who takes his worried face
And turns it upside down.
It's you who makes him bright
On the days when he feels blue.
And if you should go away,
What in heaven would he do-oo?

RICH
AND
ALL: It's you who keeps me (him) dancin'!
Who makes my (his) motor run!
Who keeps my (his) life entrancin'!
And you who keeps me (him) young, young, young!
It's you who keeps me (him) young, young, young!
It's you who keeps me (him) young, young, young!

RICH: It's you who keeps me
Agh!
Agh!

ALL: Y-O-U-N-G!

RICH: Argh!

And HE collapses to the floor.

ANGEL: Mr. Rich, are you all right?

RICH: What do you mean? Of course, I'm all right. Argh.

Falls again. Immediately, POTEMKIN rushes in with a little black doctor's bag and REVELERS come in bringing RICH's chair.

POT: All right, everybody. Just stand aside, please.

BOY: He's an old man.

ANGEL: Shhh!

BOY: But it's true. He's an old man!

Meanwhile, POTEMKIN has removed a lethal looking needle from his bag.

RICH: Wait a minute. What are you doing with that needle?

POT: Just relax the upper quandrant.

RICH: The what?

POT: Don't worry. I used to be a male nurse.

Pushes RICH over into needle position.

BOY: You were shivering when he touched you.

ANGEL: Please! If he sees us—

BOY: You were shivering. You shouldn't go with him!

RICH: Ouch! Dammit! What do you think I am? A jazz musician? What's that? What are you getting out now?

POT: *Pushing RICH back down.*

A special vibrator. It stimulates the arteries.

RICH: Oh. Good idea.

And HE lies back down for the "treatment."

ANGEL: Listen, what do you expect me to do? Get a job typing? Support the two of us?

BOY: Oh, no!

ANGEL: I tried to tell you before. I'm not gonna do that. I'm not gonna sit around and scrape and save so I can buy a copy of Vogue Magazine and look at the pictures of people who *are* somebody—I'm gonna *be* it—not just look at the pictures!

181

*Suddenly SHE stops, realizing that RICH is
right there beside them, smiling at her happily.*

RICH: What I need is a kiss from Eve. That's what I need
to bring me back to life.

*SHE looks at the BOY, and then—making up her
mind—turns to RICH and kisses him on the mouth.
Then SHE runs off, followed by the GIRLS.*
That's right, darling. You go and get ready for our
big scene.

To POTEMKIN.

What about the Adam costume?

POT: It's coming right up.

*RICH slips out of his regular clothes and down to
his long underwear.*

RICH: It's cold as a witch's tit out here.
BOY: Excuse me.—Mr. Rich. About my garden—
RICH: *Your* garden? Oh, come on. You must be kidding.
Does this look like *your* garden?
BOY: My garden is here. Underneath the earth.
RICH: Prove it.
BOY: I don't have to prove it. When the snows melt, the
seeds I planted will come up.—Thousands of them.
RICH: What makes you think so?
BOY: Because it's natural.
RICH: Natural?—It'll happen because it's "Natural"?

*And RICH laughs. HE laughs so hard, in fact,
that tears come streaming down his face.*

My! My!

Wipes his eyes.

Thank you, my boy. Thank you. I haven't had a laugh like that since I divorced my wife.—Oh, me!

Blows his nose.

Why, you homeless, half-wit, orphan idiot. All I have to do is raise my finger and all those thousands of seeds can be ripped up by machines! This garden is mine.

BOY: But you promised.

RICH: I've changed my mind. Besides, I've got a better present for you: Knowledge. Experience. The world! You don't like my values? All right. Make your own values. You don't like my falsies? Okay. Make you own. Get rid of the machines if you think you can do it. Live off flowers and love. Wonderful! But in the meantime . . . this stage is mine!

BOY: No!

RICH: Yes it is. I've worked for it. I've sweated my ass off. This is my set. My scene. My night!

Music: Ominous. Large shadows loom up in the background.

BOY: What's that?

RICH: Machines.

BOY: What are they doing?

RICH: Eating.

Music: More shadows.

You—Potemkin.

POT: Sir?

RICH: I'm going to lie down for a few minutes. All this— "exposition"—makes me weary.

Starts up steps.

183

	When the Beauticians get here—and the Body-Builders—call me.
POT:	Yes sir.
RICH:	When it's time for the New Year's Eve Pageant, call me.
POT:	Yes sir.
RICH:	And as for the kid there—Mr. "Natural"—

Pauses at the top of stairs.

Kick him out on his ass!

And RICH is gone. POTEMKIN and the Boy look at each other. The lights begin to dim. Music: as REVELERS dressed as machines appear in the shadows.

BOY:	*To POTEMKIN.*

Help me.

POT:	Why should I?
BOY:	Because you're my friend.
POT:	I didn't say that. I said I was your advisor.
BOY:	You said you'd help me!
POT:	Well, something went wrong. The trick got screwed up!
BOY:	You know what to do. You said so. "Somebody older—wiser—a little bit more experienced in the—"
POT:	Listen, I want to tell you a little secret. I used to be a preacher.
BOY:	You did?
POT:	Yes. I was a very holy man. Compassionate. Committed. I took the problems of the world and put them right there—right on my shoulders. And then

one day I found out that God is dead. So you know what I did? I look at the world around me and I said OK. OK.

Music: POTEMKIN begins to sing as REVEL-ERS in machine costumes sing and dance with him.

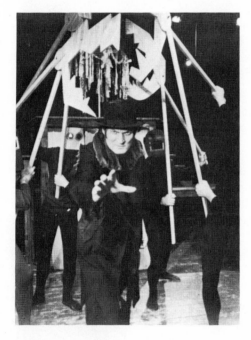

Oslo, Norway, Riksteatret production: PER SKIFT as Potemkin.

The Earth is being eaten by machines.
Not my problem.
(Not his problem)
Taking "speed" can re-arrange your genes.
Not my problem.
(Not his problem)

God is dead
That's what they said.
I read it in an interview.
If it's so
I'd like to know
Just what the hell am I supposed to do?

I'd like to see us all
Become like saints.
But since that cannot be—
Then it's simply not my
Pro-o-o-o-blem!

*Machines dance. Strange, delicate. A sort of creaking
minuet, rather like something out of Disney's "Fan-
tasia."*

The Chinese have a nuclear device.
Not my problem.
(Not his problem)
Every politician has his price.
Not my problem.
(Not his problem)

I've become
A humble bum:
A drop-out from humanity.
You may think
My morals stink,
But at least I keep my sanity.
I know the world will
Soon be going "boom!"
Despite what we may do.
But it's simply not my
Pro-o-o-o-blem!

Machines dance.

POT : *Slower and more menacing.*

Somebody screams in terror on the street.
Not my problem!
(Not his problem)
People die of hunger; I repeat:
Not my problem!
(Not his problem)

God is dead.
That's what they said.
Done in by Darwin, Marx and Freud.
Free are we
From Diety.
Of course it sort of leaves a little void.

I used to care about my fellow man.
But now—hurrah—I'm free.
And it's simply not my problem!

BOY : All right, if you won't help me, I'll do it on my own.
POT : Do what? What are you going to do?
BOY : Fight him.
POT : *What?*

Laughing.

Oh, come on!
BOY : Look at me!
POT : You'll never win, kid. He's old and smart.
BOY : I said: Look at me!
POT : He knows all the tricks. He's been around a long
time.
BOY : The sun!
The sun!

The sun!
POT: Some people say that today is the day
When the cold will come
And never
Go away . . .
BOY: God made the sun.
And the sun made light.
And the light, cut in two,
Made day and night . . .
POT: Some people say that tonight is the night
When the bird will fly
And eat away the light . . .
BOY: God had a dream.
And the dream came true.
And the dream, cut in two,
Was me and you.
Me and you. . . .
Me and you. . . .

And now the Music becomes more excited, almost feverish, as the BOY pleads his case.

Fifty million years ago
Something in the sea
Reached above the water eagerly!

Fifty thousand years ago
Something on the land
Suddenly decided it could stand!
Does this lonely road just go to nowhere?
Can it be that there's no reason why?
When in spite of all the strife
And the endless dying,
Life keeps reaching higher
For the sky!

Fifty seconds from right now
Anything can be!
I'm the future.
Please—believe in me!

Anything we need—
Anything we long for—
Anything we dream
Can come to be!

POT: *As Music continues.*

Hey, hey, hey.—What are you so happy about, all of a sudden?

BOY: I'm not going to leave. I'm going to stay! I'm going to fight him—for the girl. For the garden. For everything!

And RICH suddenly screams on the upper platform.

RICH: Aaieee!
POT: Oh my God, what was that?
BOY: The future belongs to me! I'm going to make a new world! I'm going to correct all of the mistakes he made. I'm going to make it perfect!

Sings.

Fifty seconds from right now
Anything can be.
I'm the future.
Please—believe in me!

Anything we need—
Anything we long for—
Anything we dream
Can come to be:

Believe!
You will see!
It can come—
To be!

RICH screams.

POT: *Looks back and forth, from one to the other. Then:*

All right. But remember. I go with the winner.
Either way.

The boy rushes off and RICH screams.

All right. Stop the yelling.

And HE rushes up steps.

What's the matter with you, anyway? You sound
like a human sacrifice. Ugh!

*This last because RICH has suddenly risen and
grabbed him by the throat.*

RICH: I was having a nightmare!
I dreamt of a girl—
A young girl—

POT: She's downstairs. Getting into her fig leaf for the
party.

RICH: It was very warm.
And the insides of my hands
Were sweaty.
I could feel the perspiration
Streaming—down—down—

POT: Perhaps you'd like to see the Youth Consultant.

RICH: The girl was hot, too.
It was is if it was Summer

And we were both of us
On fire.
And so I reached out
And I grabbed her!
But then—suddenly—
Instead of her
I was holding in my arms
A mannequin.
It was shaped like her, you see—
But it wasn't flesh and blood.
It was sculpted
Out of ice!
So that my tongue got stuck
Onto the ice-tongue,
And my arms got grafted
Around her stomach.
And I was caught there—
Eee!
Freezing to death
While squeezed
Into an amorous embrace!
Agh!

Shudders violently. Then turns to POTEMKIN.

	What about the Boy?
POT:	He's locked out.
RICH:	Good. What about the Beauticians?
REVEL:	*Dressed as BEAUTICIANS.*
	Here!
RICH:	Barbers?
REVEL:	*Dressed as BARBERS.*
	Here!

RICH: Body-builders?
REVEL: *Dressed as BODY-BUILDERS.*

Here!
RICH: What about my costume—for the ball?
REVEL: *Running in with glittering costume.*

Here!

RICH takes costume and begins to slip into it with the aid of the others. The REVELER who brought it in lowers his mask and we see that it is the BOY.
POT: Oh my God!
RICH: *Still dressing.*

Did you call me?
POT: No. I said "good." About your costume!
BOY: Where is she? I can't find her.
POT: What are you trying to do—ruin me?—Hide!

And HE manages to get the BOY out of sight just before RICH stands up in his completed costume.

RICH: All right, men. Now hear this!

Music.

Your assignment is to make me young again—to take this flabby old flesh and make it taut and pink and succulent—to turn me from the Heavy into the Juvenile Lead!
Sings.

It's you who makes me young
When I start feeling old.
It's you who makes me lovely
When I cross your palm with gold.

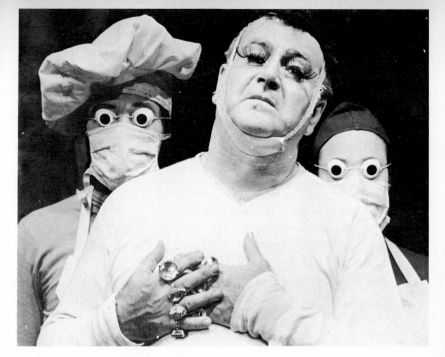

BEAUT: And when the seasons change
And the winter's on its way,
We will make you young as spring:
All you have to do is pa-ay!
It's us: it's us who makes you young.
Massage!
Mudpack!
Girdle!
Facial!
Chin-strap!
Toupee!
Stuff, Squeeze,
Paint, Tease!
Push, Rub,
Cover, Shove!
Grab, Snap,
Tap, Slap!
Pull, Glue,
Pin, Screw!

193

RICH: *Speaking over the Music.*

What about the doctors?

POT: Coming right up!

And the DOCTOR MASKS rush up to the upper platform, carrying a little black bags and huge "commedia" needles. ONE of them lifts his mask. It is the BOY.

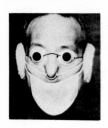

POT: Oh, no.

RICH: What's the matter? Who are you talking to?

POT: *To the BOY.*

Quick. Behind the curtain. Hurry!

RICH: —*Ouch!*

This last because POTEMKIN gives him the needle full force and then pushes the BOY out of sight.

POT: *Gasping—points to RICH.*

Oh my God, you look like—!

RICH: Who?

POT: Like the young boy. Like the hero!

RICH: I don't believe you!

POT: Look in the mirror!

194

Pulls down drape in front of the Boy. RICH swoons. The BOY does the same. RICH gets up. The BOY follows. Then as the Music picks up "Once Upon a Time" RICH does a ballet. Or, more accurately, RICH and the BOY do a ballet together. It is a delicate Love-Dance. A dance of Narcissus, as RICH and the YOUNG BOY dance in and out of the mirror frames, reflecting alter-images of an ego.

RICH: *Sings.*

Oh can it be me-me-me?
Those little locks so fine.
Those teeth that really shine!

195

TED THURSTON as Rich and MICHAEL GLENN-SMITH as the Boy, Broadway production.

BEAUT: *Sing.*
Yes it is you!
Yes it is true!

RICH: I can't believe this face I see
Is really me.
I'm twenty-three.

And, joyously, RICH continues his dance. Only this time, as HE turns to see his image in the mirror, HE sees instead a grisly spectre dressed in white and carrying a scythe and an hour glass.

SPECTRE: "There is nothing more certain
Than the sweeping scythe of Time!"

RICH: Who the hell are you?

POT: *Lowering the white beard.*

It's me, Mr. Rich. Potemkin. I'm supposed to be Father Time. It's part of the entertainment—for New Year's Eve.

RICH: Oh. Well, don't scare me like that. You'll make my pants split.

A gong is struck. RICH jumps nervously.

What the hell is going on now?

POT: It's time for the pageant. It's almost midnight.

RICH: Well, tell 'em to take it easy, will you? My toupee's slipping.

A GIRL rushes in, gives RICH champagne and a little New Year's Eve noise maker, and helps him to his special viewing position, down near the audience.

RICH: *To Audience.*

Can you see all right?—Tell me if I get in the way. Okay?

POT: *As FATHER TIME, speaks in elaborate, fruity,*
"carnival" voice.

Ladies and gentlemen—
Children—
Parents—
Old—
Young—
Rich—
Poor—
Lovers—
Haters—
All, in fact,
Who live and die—
And are thus
The humble subjects
Of the great god—Time.
In this moment—as the old year passes—
We present—
A lively pageant
Depicting "New Year's Eve in Many Lands"

Bong.

RICH: *Yells out.*

Take it easy on that gong!
POT: Sorry.
RICH: And cut out some of the crap. Get on to the dancing.
POT: Right.

Then back to his fruity voice.

Part one:
"The Seasons"
Attend thee
To Assyria!

197

The ancient Snake Dance
Of the sacred god Ashur.

Music: Middle Eastern music as FOUR SEDUC-TIVE NEAR-NAKED MAIDENS slither out onto the platform.

RICH: Yeah! That's more like it.

Applauds.

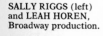

POT: First
The new-born season:
Spring!
The season of hope and captivating innocence.
And the YOUNGEST of the FOUR MAIDENS moves forward and dances.

Second
The sunlit season:
Summer!
The fecund season of the rich, round belly of desire.

SUMMER MAIDEN does belly dance right in front of RICH's face.

Third
The bitter-sweet season:
Autumn!
The season of harvest and remembrance.

Third dance.

And last of all
Resplendent in its clarity
The season of the bleached bones:
Winter!

SALLY RIGGS (left)
and **LEAH HOREN**,
Broadway production.

CINDI BULAK (left)
and KEITH CHARLES.

*And the last MAIDEN removes her veil—to show
us, behind it, a grinning death mask.*

RICH: Hey. What the hell kind of stripper is that?
POT: That's the ultimate stripper, Mr. Rich. The grim stripper.
RICH: Well, get her out of here.
POT: Right.

MAIDEN runs off.

POT: Part Two:
"The Saturnalia!"
Attend thee further
As Father Time whisks you forward through the centuries
To the Roman New Year: the Saturnalia!

Music: Wild and sensual as REVELERS step forward in costumes reminiscent of Mardi-Gras.

POT: *Over the Music.*

As the Romans reached the New Year,
They spent their time in carnival:
In revelling and feasts
And mad pursuit of pleasure.
REVEL: *Sing.*

SATURNALIA!
SATURNALIA!
SATURNALIA!
SATURNALIA!
POT: They selected a slave
To act as Mock-King
And rule over the wild debauch.

Left to right: PAMELA PEADON,
STEPHEN de GHELDER as the Mock King,
and SALLY RIGGS, Broadway production.

A *huge puppet figure appears and ascends to the upper platform. HE bears an uncanny resemblance to RICH.*

REVEL: SATURNALIA!
SATURNALIA!
SATURNALIA!
SATURNALIA!

POT: See the Mock-King
In his fine attire!

And we see upon the MOCK-KING's fingers the same rings that RICH wears.

See the Mock-King
Take his pleasure
With the slave girls!

And we see the MOCK-KING embrace a GIRL dressed very much like ANGEL.

See the Mock-King eat!

And we see the MOCK-KING eat the same lobster that RICH ate in Act One.

Left to right: NORMAN MATHEWS, FRANK NEWELL, STEPHEN deGHELDER as the Mock King, FELIX RICE, and GARY WALES, Broadway production.

See the Mock-King drink!
See the Mock-King dance!
See the Mock-King die!

And THEY cut his head off.

RICH: *Jumping up.*

What the hell is going on around here? I told you not to startle me!

POT: I'm sorry, Mr. Rich. But the Mock-King has to die. That's part of the ritual.

RICH: Well, all right. So kill him. But don't make it so noisy!

POT: Yes, sir.
"Attend thee—"

RICH: And lay off that "Attend thee" crap. Come on. Let's get to the love scene. Bring the girl out. "Woman! Woman!"

POT: But Mr. Rich, she isn't ready.

RICH: What do you mean, isn't ready? It's almost midnight.

POT: Her hand-maidens are still preparing her. She's in the harem.

RICH: The what?

POT: She's being purified to receive the blessings of my Lord Krishna. Ooops. Sorry. I mean—Adam.

RICH: Oh.—Well, can I talk to her, at least?

POT: Of course.

Claps his hands.

But remember: No peeking.

Music: Mysterious and vaguely "Eastern" as the

"hand-maidens" appear, tittering and giggling. THEY slowly unwind the cocoon of silk from ANGEL's shoulders, holding it up at strategic points to shield her partly clothed body from RICH's eyes.

RICH: Is she there?

POTEMKIN nods, so RICH yells over the wall of silk.

Yoo-hoo.—I'm young again. And handsome. So you believe me?

Suddenly the silk parts and the BOY appears beside ANGEL, unseen by RICH. SHE looks intently at his face.

ANGEL: I do. Yes.

RICH: My chin, for example. I had them put some volcanic mud on that. It makes my chin look young again.

ANGEL: It's beautiful.

RICH: What's that?

ANGEL: *Reaching out her hand to touch the BOY's face.*

It's like a piece of marble. Like a sculpture by Michelangelo.

RICH: *Feeling chin.*

Really? Well, I certainly hired the best I could get. And say—my hair—

ANGEL: It's soft and golden.

RICH: Golden?

ANGEL: . . . and it smells fresh and musty at the same time.

RICH: It does?

Takes off toupee. Smells.

Phew!

ANGEL: And your shoulders are strong.

RICH: What's that again?

ANGEL: And your hands are brown and rough from working in the outside.

RICH: Could you speak a little louder? I'm having some difficulty in hearing all that.

ANGEL: *To the BOY.*

I said—you're beautiful.

RICH: *Faints.*

Agh!

ANGEL: And I want you to be part of me.

RICH: Oh, God!

Tries to break through veil, but POTEMKIN holds him back.

Yes! That's what I want, too! To be part of you! *Yes!*
Part of you!

To POTEMKIN.

Come on. I'm ready for the Love Scene. Do the cue,

POT: But Mr. Rich, you don't want to push too hard. You heard what the doctor said. It's dangerous.

RICH: Dangerous? Of course it's dangerous. Suppose I crawl inside my bed and pull the cover over my head. That wouldn't be dangerous, would it?

POT: Well, I . . .

RICH: Suppose I joined the Old Folk's home and was wheeled around all day by an attendant with bad breath. That wouldn't be dangerous either. Come on. Start the music, like I told you.

To ANGEL, through veil.

Listen. Can you hear me? We're gonna do the Love Scene now.

And the Music picks up Love Song in the background.

ANGEL: *To the BOY shaking her head.*

It'll never work out. We're too different.

RICH: Don't say that. Please!

ANGEL: *To the BOY.*

This is a Masquerade. It's Make-Believe. The real world isn't like this.

RICH: Then we'll change the real world.

ANGEL: It's not that easy. Believe me.

RICH: It's the life force. That's what counts! You've got to throw yourself into the fire! Can you hear me?

ANGEL: *By now the BOY has begun to kiss her.*

Yes, yes!—The Fire!

RICH: Don't be afraid of the consequences. Give in! Surrender!

ANGEL: *A low moan as the BOY embraces her.*

I can't! I can't!

RICH: Yes, you can!

Sings.

Love Song!

BOY: *Sings.*

Love Song!

Seattle, Washington, A Contemporary T production: CAROLE DEMAS as and MICHAEL GLENN-SMITH as th

204

BOTH: Love Song!
RICH: *To POTEMKIN.*

        All right. I'm ready for the love scene. Do the cue.
        "Woman."
POT: "And so the new dawn brought forth Woman.
        Out of the slumber rose she—
        Her hair the color of peacock's feathers.
        Her brow like ivory.
        Her two bright eyes like lotuses.
        Like the eyes of a gazelle."
RICH: This is Eve?
POT: Shh.

        Then HE continues.

        "Her swelling breasts bore two dark points—
        Trim as a lance stood her supple young body.
        Her legs were like the stretched out trunks
        Of elephants."
RICH: Elephants? Her legs were like elephants?
POT: Shh.
        "She was glowing with little delicate pearls.
        Of perspiration.
        And when Brahma became aware of her,
        He arose from his Yogic posture—"
RICH: Brahma? Yogic?
POT: It's all the same thing. Believe me.
RICH: What is?
POT: Woman. New Year. The chance of birth and love.
        It's all the same thing.
RICH: All right—all right. So do the cue, for heaven's sake!
POT: Part three

<pre>
            Eve!—
            Under the tree!—
            Aphrodite!
RICH: *Aphrodite?*
POT: The Corn Goddess!
            Juno!
            Cocoa Mama!
            Mother Earth!
RICH: Oh, for God's sake!
POT: Woman!
</pre>

The GIRL comes in nude. As the REVELERS grab up bits of cloth and tinsel to make a huge, living "tree" of bodies, she kneels before them and sings.

<pre>
ANGEL: Under the tree,
            Under the tree,
            Down where the leaves billow—billow—

            Under the tree,
            Under the tree,
            There is a green pillow—pillow—
</pre>

SUSAN WATSON as Angel with Revelers, Broadway production.

I know the way;
Follow me, follow me.
Don't be afraid:
Follow me, follow me.
Give me your hand.
Un-do my hair,
Open my heart,
Take me!
Take me!

Under the tree,
Under the tree,
Down where the leaves billow—billow,
Under the tree,
Make love to me.

*Music continues, lush and sensual, as ANGEL does
a seductive dance, the BOY appears, unseen by
RICH. He is naked also, and he and the girl dance
together.*

REVEL
(GIRLS): *Sing.*

Flesh of my flesh God made you—
Made you a part of my very inside.
Flesh of my flesh God made you—
So we could be together for life.

Breathe and I know you are breathing.
Die, and I think I would die.
Grieve and my own heart starts grieving.
You and I—we are one person.

Flesh of my flesh, God made you—

Clockwise: SU
SON as Angel,
GLENN-SM
Boy, KEITH CI
Potemkir
THURSTON as
folio Workshop p

Part of my own inside.
And we must stay forever—
Side by side—
Side by side—
Side by side.

ANGEL: Under the tree.
Under the tree.
Down where the leaves
Billow—billow—

Under the tree
Make love to me.

*And at the end of it, the young BOY and the girl
embrace, and RICH realizes that he has been
tricked.*

RICH: Hey! Hey! What the hell is going on here?
POT: *As FATHER TIME.*

"And now, ladies and gentlemen—
The grand finale!"

RICH: You were supposed to keep him out of here!
POT: *Please!* This is the big number. The climax!
RICH: I don't care what it is. You told me . . .
POT: But Mr. Rich, we can't stop now. It's almost mid-
night.
RICH: No, no, no, no!
POT: The show's nearly finished. The clock is ticking.
Part four.
The Grand Finale!
A Ritual Battle.
Between Winter and Summer.

208

The old Year and the New!

Ladies and Gentlemen—
For your amusement—
A battle unto death!

*Music: As the REVELERS start singing, TWO
DANCERS clad in ancient masks and armor step
forward on the upper platform, duplicating the posi-
tions of the boy and the old man, down below.*

REVEL: *Sing.*

Winter and summer
Fire and cold.
See how they battle;
Young against the old!

Program cover for the
Stadteater production,
Helsingborgs, Sweden.

ANGEL steps forward. The boy and the old man rush forward and begin to plead their case.

RICH: I can give you anything you want! You name it: Money. Jewels. Possessions!

BOY: I can give you the Future.

RICH: He doesn't have a thing.

BOY: My hands are warm.

RICH: You'll never be Somebody. Not with him!

BOY: I'm young!

RICH: He's nobody. Nobody!

BOY: I'm young!

You understand?

He's old. I'm young!

He's dying! I'm alive!

POT: *As FATHER TIME.*

Choose.

SHE turns to the BOY—reaches out to him. But the OLD MAN won't allow it.

RICH: No!

And wildly, almost insanely, HE rushes forward and snatches ANGEL from his rival. As the boy and the old man struggle on the lower level for the possession of the GIRL, the two masked DANCERS duplicate their battle on the upper platform in slow, ritualistic motion.

REVEL: *Sing.*

Winter and summer.
Death versus birth.
See how they struggle
To possess the Earth!

Placard designs by HS.

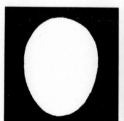 

*And now the battle reaches its climax as RICH, in
an almost superhuman effort, pushes the BOY down
and grabs the girl, while on the upper platform the
two masked dancers climax their battle.*

RICH: *Dragging the girl forward to the very center of the
upper platform.*

She's mine, do you understand? She's mine! I defy
you, Father Time. I defy all of you. This is my
scene! *My* moment! *My* Night!—What's the matter?—Where is everybody going?—What's it so
quiet for?

*And slowly, very slowly, POTEMKIN dressed as
FATHER TIME, lifts his hand and ONE of the
REVELERS appears in a faceless white mask holding a mirror on a pole. In the distance, a gong is
softly struck.*

POT: *Softly.*

One.

*And there is heard suddenly a strange "popping"
sound.*

RICH: What's the noise?
ANGEL: Mr. Rich—your girdle—
RICH: What about my girdle?
ANGEL: It's popping.
RICH: Oh my God!

POTEMKIN signals. Again the clock sounds.

POT: Two.

RICH reaches behind to try and stop the popping. This makes his toupee fall off. HE bends down to pick it up. RIP. The sleeves tear.

RICH: Agh!

HE tries to repair it. Toupee falls again.

Help me!

POTEMKIN signals. Clock strikes. Another faceless REVELER with another mirror.

POT: Three.

RICH reaches for toupee. Zop. The pants fall. HE grabs for them. ZIP! Another tear. HE's literally coming to pieces in front of our eyes. The GIRL, who has been standing beside him, pulls away in horror.

RICH: No. Wait. I can get it fixed.

HE stumbles forward, but ANGEL pulls away and rushes over to the BOY. POTEMKIN signals. The clock strikes. Another REVELER and mirror appear.

POT: Four.
RICH: Just a minute, I'm not ready.
Don't bring the mirrors yet!
POT: Five.
RICH: Wait a minute, I told you.
I won't look! I refuse.
Take away the mirrors!

As HE catches sight of himself.

Agh!

POTEMKIN signals. The clock strikes. Another mirror.

POT: Six.
RICH: Oh God—
Who is that?
That old man?
Ugh.
He's horrible.

POTEMKIN signals. The clock strikes, Another mirror. THEY are closing in all around him now.

213

POT : Seven.
RICH : Look at him :
Burnt-out.
Hollow.
A clown—
A sad old clown.

Suddenly.

That isn't me!

POTEMKIN signals. The clock strikes. Another mirror appears.

POT : Eight.
RICH : Oh no.
That's me—over there.
That's my face.

Goes to BOY.

Look at it!!

POTEMKIN signals. The clock strikes. Another mirror appears.

POT : Nine.
RICH : Innocent.
Fresh.
Look at that "possibility."

POTEMKIN signals. The clock strikes. Another mirror appears.

POT : Ten.
RICH : I'm gonna change the world!
I've got my whole life still ahead of me!

POTEMKIN signals. The clock strikes. Another mirror.

Seattle, Washington, A Contemporary Theatre
production: CAROLE DEMAS as Angel
and MICHAEL GLENN-SMITH as the Boy.

POT: Eleven.

RICH: *To the BOY.*

I am you, don't you see?
You are me.
We are the same thing . . .

*HE tries to keep talking, but there is no more
sound. HE looks at the rest of them, astonished.*

POTEMKIN signals. The clock strikes Softly.

POT: Twelve.

*And now, even the soundless jaw stops moving. The
OLD MAN slumps as the last of the faceless faces
appears carrying a mirror on a pole.*

*Suddenly there is a distant explosion of sound:
drums and rattles and little New Year's Eve party
favors and whistles. Then, just as suddenly as it had
come, the hollow sounds die down and, fitfully, disappear.*

*One by one, the REVELERS remove their masks
so that we see their faces for the first time. Then—
all of them—the whole company—peers out into the
darkness of the Auditorium.*

BOY: What's out there? Do you know? Out there in the
streets? Outside the theatre?

ANGEL: The world. The *real* world.

BOY: *Squinting his eyes.*

It's dark, isn't it?

ANGEL: It's grey.

BOY: The air is being poisoned.

215

ANGEL: Half of the people are starving.
BOY: We're destroying the other animals.
ANGEL: People don't know what to believe in anymore.

Pause. SHE looks at him.

I'll never be Somebody, will I?

HE shakes his head. SHE smiles sadly.

The "Golden Goddess!"
BOY: The garden is gone, isn't it?

SHE nods. HE looks around.

I'm going to miss it, in a way. You could always count on it. You know?

Drumbeat. It grows darker.

ANGEL: Are you afraid?
BOY: Yes.
ANGEL: So am I.

And gravely—very gravely—HE offers her his hand. And SHE takes it. THEY go to POTEM- KIN and kneel before him. Music begins under.

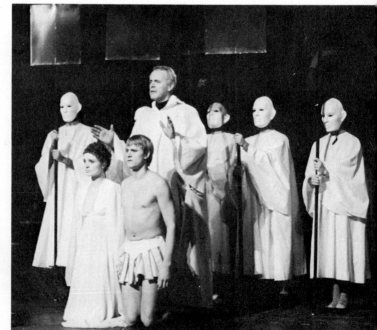

Odense, Denmark, Odense Teater production, left to right: LANE LIND as Angel, OLE MOLLEGAARD as the Boy, PREBEN BORGGAARD as Potemkin.

POT: In this time of cold and darkness—
In this terrifying night—
In this seemingly endless Winter,
Let us pray that they'll be all right.

*BOY and GIRL rise and, hand in hand, THEY
go down the aisle and out the door of the theatre
and into the street. As THEY do so, ONE BY
ONE, the REVELERS, led by POTEMKIN,
begin to sing, and light after light comes pouring on
at EVERYONE holds up images of the sun.*

ALL: *Sing.*

Some people say
That today is the day
When the cold will come
And never go away.
When the bird will fly,
The wind will blow,
But something deep inside me says it can't be so.
I want to celebrate!
Make a celebration!
I want to celebrate!
Savor each sensation.
Something deep inside
(Something deep inside)
Says "beneath the snow"
(Says "beneath the snow.")
"There's a tiny seed."
("There's a tiny seed.")
"And it's gonna grow!"
("And it's gonna grow!")

217

I want to celebrate
Every day! Every day!
Every day! Every day!
Every day! Every day!
Every day! Every day!
Make a celebration—
Every day!
Celebration!

The large sun above the platform moves out of the eclipse and becomes the full sun. And the play is done.

Footnotes

by Tom Jones

TOM JONES (left) and HARVEY SCHMIDT (right) in the costume room of Portfolio Workshop.

The Fantasticks

It is strange about *THE FANTASTICKS*. Harvey and I worked on it off and on for years as a big musical for Broadway. We had set the charming little Rostand story realistically in two adjoining ranches in the Southwest. We had cowboys, Mexican bandits, and even a half-breed villain. But the whole thing wouldn't work. It just wouldn't come together. And besides, it seemed pompous and archaic.

Then in the Spring of 1959, several things happened in rapid succession. (1) I fell in love. Blindly. Wildly. Stupidly. I experienced again all those terrible sweet agonies of romantic passion. But I wasn't really *that* young anymore, and I couldn't help but laugh at myself even as I felt the rapture and the pain. I wrote in a letter to the girl "You are Polaris, the one true star!" And I meant it. But I saw that it was funny too. (2) Two theatrical events occurred which set my imagination on fire. One was the film of *The Seventh Seal,* which I saw for the first time in the late fifties, and which featured a small band of actors travelling in a wagon during medevial times. The other influence was a production by the Piccolo Theatro di Milano of *Servant of Two Masters* done on a platform as if by a troup of itinerant Commedia players. Something in these two visions of the theatre —the small band of players, the simple platform, the use of imagination instead of scenery—something in all this fascinated both Harvey and me and turned us on. (3) Word Baker, our friend and co-worker since college days (after all, we had done *HIPSY BOO* together), was offered the opportunity to stage

223

three new one act plays at a summer theatre that
Mildred Dunnock was opening at Barnard College
in New York City. Word wanted one of them to be
a musical. So he offered us a challenge. If we could
reduce the Rostand piece to one act and write it in
three weeks, Word would guarantee us a production
three weeks after that. The results were amazing.
After five years of piddling and plodding, we threw
out the huge, complex book and score and, starting
with the premise of a platform, we wrote what was
the substance of *THE FANTASTICKS* in three
weeks.

It was, as I say, strange. And we were lucky. And
although it would be very foolish to generalize too
much upon such a particular and unusual method of
creation, several things became apparent to us which
were to form the basis for almost all of our later
thinking. First: "Less is more." Compression. Re-
striction. These are, paradoxically, the keys to re-
lease and freedom. The imagination is stifled by
too much "stuff." The theatre works best, like dance,
when it is at its barest. Second: "There are no
rules." Or rather, the rules are different in each case.
When we sat down to write *THE FANTAS-
TICKS* in three weeks, we decided to break all the
"rules." After all, what the hell, what did we have
to lose? And finally, the last thing I learned from
THE FANTASTICKS, I didn't learn right away.
It took me years, in fact. And years. And it was the
most important thing of all. Namely, you have to be
in love. If not with some*one,* then with some*thing.*
Not all the skill in the world, not all the knowledge,
not all the daring means anything at all in your
writing if you are not passionately in love.

Celebration

"What should I say when it is better to say nothing?"

That old folk saying comes vividly to mind as I sit to write these notes. How I love Shakespeare. He is my hero. My god. I love his language; I love his people; I love his craft. And I also love the fact that his plays are so honest-plain upon the printed page. No prefaces. No stage directions. No helpful notes to tell you what he had in mind. What is there is there. What you see you see. How awful if he had "explained" Hamlet. Or Lear. He created them. It is up to others to explain them.

THE FANTASTICKS doesn't have too many notes and stage directions either. Of course I don't pretend that it approaches in any way the quality of Shakespeare, but at least it looks a little bit like Shakespeare on the page. It is in verse, most of it, and it leaves lots of space on the sides, and I like that.

CELEBRATION is different. For one thing, it is mostly in prose. For another, it requires a bit more explanation. It is "different" from other musicals. In fact, I'm not even sure it is a "musical" at all. Not in the usual sense of the word. It is a fable. It has ritual overtones. It is based upon ancient ceremonies depicting the battle between Winter and Summer. It was suggested by an editorial in the New York *Times* about the meaning of the Winter Solstice. It annoyed the hell out of some people. It delighted others. It ran for only 109 performances on Broadway. But it is done often around the country and the world. And it has been phenomenally successful in Scandanavia (where the Winter Solstice is something to be reckoned with.)

I had intended to write a long explanation of my feelings about *CELEBRATION,* but I don't think I will do that, after all. Here is the text. It has many flaws, but it has many virtues too. And both the flaws and the virtues are personal ones. I like Mr. Rich and Potemkin. They are my heroes. I like the score too, especially the music.

We did *CELEBRATION* first at our Portfolio studio. It felt good there. It belonged. When we moved it into the Ambassador Theatre on Broadway, it didn't feel as good. It seemed somewhat silly up there, not because it was less effective than a Broadway musical, but because it *wasn't* a Broadway musical. Who knows? Perhaps we will do it again someday. With revisions. And in a proper place.

TOM JONES (left) and **HARVEY SCHMIDT** (right) photographed at Portfolio Workshop.

226

Portfolio: A Dream

In 1966, with *I DO, I DO* and *FANTAS-TICKS* both running in New York at the same time, Harvey and I set out to find a theatre of our own. It had been our dream since 1950 when we had started working together in college. Now was the time. We knew that. If we didn't do our "own thing" now, we would got too established. Too "fat." Too scared.

And so we found an old building which had once been a chapel for immigrant weddings and we converted it with the expert help of our business manager, Bob Gold, into a working theatre space. Harvey designed a stage. We begged and borrowed costumes and props from wherever we could get them. We invited a few actor friends to join us and then we began professional classes in circus techniques and belly dancing as well as exercises and experiments having to do with masks, mirrors and mockery.

227

It has been five years now since the Portfolio experiment actually got underway. It has produced three pieces so far: *CELEBRATION,* which was later done on Broadway and which is included in this volume; *PHILEMON,* a musical play about the crucifixion of a clown in Roman times; and *RATFINK,* which is the story of a middle-aged man who glues bones in the Museum of Natural History. All three are originals. All three have been written for the same stage (our unit set at Portfolio). The last two have as yet only been seen by small groups of invited guests, but it is our hope to complete one or two more original pieces and then open the entire body of work to the public.

We have learned a great deal during these five years. We have made so many mistakes. My God, it is easy to be pompous. Easy to be dull. We have searched for the meaning of ritual theatre. We have tried to combine Peter Brooks "holy" theatre with "popular" theatre. We have worked with masks, with crude musical instruments from around the world. We have tried a rough form of "communion," both among the actors and then later among the invited audiences. (I would hate to guess how many gallons of Almaden burgundy have been guzzled down during that noble experiment.)

At the end of it all, I have some very definite and strong feelings about "ritual" theatre. About its possibilities, and about its dangers and its limitations too. A few years ago, wildly excited and impressed by photographs of the Bread and Puppet Theatre, I finally saw them in action. I was fascinated. But disturbed too. Depressed. Something was missing. Something important. What was it? I sat down and

made the following notes to myself. [Some of them
are in verse form because that is the way I usually
write when I get excited.] The notes ramble a bit,
but I think they pretty well sum up what I feel now
about this whole experiment with ritual.

SOME THOUGHTS AFTER SEEING
THE BREAD AND PUPPET THEATRE

We instinctively reject the "prose" theatre.
The theatre of "doors" and "chairs."
Of telephones ringing.
Of cigarettes.
Of slyly interjected "exposition."
Further
We reject "unimportant" theatre.
Fascile theatre.
What we have come to think of
As "commercial" theatre.
Theatre which is motivated primarily by a desire
For success rather than by a desire of self-expression
For group revelation.

And this rejection of the cheap side of the commercial theatre leads us too often to a rejection of
"entertainment" per se.

As in Grotowski:
No laughter during class.
No laughter during rehearsals.
No laughter during performance.

Like a church.
No laughter.
As though laughter were the enemy
Of revelation.

As though laughter were not, in fact,
Perhaps the ultimate revelation.

Tears without laughter
Is like laughter without tears:
Either one is essentially shallow.
A half-experience.
A half-vision.

Put the two together:
Not the mask of comedy
And
The mask of tragedy,

But as one face,
Twisting—

Impossible opposites
Irrevocably joined together.

Do that
And then we have made some progress.

And so—
To the Bread and Puppet Theatre.

Its origins:
Ritual
Group experience.
Symbolic theatre.

Good.
No. Better than good.
Wonderful.
Marvelous.
Important.

A view.
A vision.

Of the theatre
Too long neglected.

But at what a price!

If this theatre,
Non-verbal,
Symbolic,
Masked,
And ritualized,
Is meant to replace
The theatre of man,
Of man's anguish
And hilarity,
His god-head
And stupidity—

If man's intricate, inexorable, unexpected humanity
Is to be replaced (exclusively)
By Bread and Puppets—
By solemn figures
Ten feet tall.
Inhuman
Savagely symbolic
But frozen:
Attitudinized
Immobile
Expectable
(The very opposite of man)

Then I say
No!
And again No!
And once more
No.

It will not do.

A ritual theatre, yes!
And puppets, yes!
And bread
And wine
And sacraments
And symbolic essences
Enacted for our own ennobling

Yes to all this.

BUT NOT WITHOUT MAN!

NOT WITHOUT HUMANITY!

NOT WITHOUT THE INDIVIDUAL
SOUL!

Throw out the telephones!
Throw out the sofas
And the doorframes
And the flats
And the exposition.
And the fascile.
And the expected.

Go dangerous.
Go deep.
Go new.
(And old too)

Incantation?
By all means.
And ritual.
And prayer.

Dispense with "stories" (plots)
If they seem too comfortable.

Avoid novelty.
Seek grace.

Have puppets, masks,
The whole works

But, for God's sakes,
Please—
Not without man.
And remember this:
Ritual, for all its virtues,
(And they are many
And I espouse them)
Ritual can become rote—
Its original life forces
Harden
Like coral on a reef.

Like mumbled incantations.
In a foreign tongue.

There is an ancient comfort in ritual.
But without the living heart
Without the immediacy of you and me,
Of us,
Of we,
In other words,
Without humanity—

Ritual is dead.
And deadly.

And it is a death more dead than those traditional
prose plays against which we all rebel.

London production: JUNE RITCHIE as Luisa.